MY JAPAN

A Cultural Memoir

ALSO BY ROGER PULVERS

Liv
Half of Each Other
The Honey and the Fires
The Dream of Lafcadio Hearn
Peaceful Circumstances
The Unmaking of an American

Roger Pulvers

MY JAPAN

A Cultural Memoir

BALESTIER PRESS
LONDON · SINGAPORE

Balestier Press
Centurion House, London TW18 4AX
www.balestier.com

My Japan: A Cultural Memoir
Copyright © Roger Pulvers, 2020

First published by Balestier Press in 2020

A CIP catalogue record for this book
is available from the British Library.

ISBN 978 1 911221 79 1

This is the original, revised and updated edition of *If There Were No Japan* [Moshi nihon to iu kuni ga nakattara], published in Japanese translation in 2011 by Shueisha International, Tokyo, and subsequently in English by Japan Publishing Industry Foundation for Culture.

Japanese names appearing in this book are given in Japanese order, with family name first. In some cases, in accordance with Japanese usage, a famous person may be referred to by their given name only.

All translations appearing in this book are by Roger Pulvers.

Cover illustration by Alice Pulvers

All rights reserved. No part of this publication may be reproduced, stored in a retrieval system or transmitted in any form or by any means, electronic, mechanical, without the prior written permission of the publisher of this book.

Contents

Preface *7*

Part One

1. This Is My Country *15*
2. The Puzzle Comes Together to Form a Picture *35*
3. Responsibility for the Past *47*
4. Complete Imperfection *57*
5. The Five Japans *75*
6. Miraculous Moments *89*
7. A Dialogue with the Japanese People *105*
8. Like the Fish Who Live in the Depths of the Sea *117*

Part Two

9. Becoming Acclimatized to the Wind and the Earth *141*
10. Overturning the Past *145*
11. A Labyrinth of Color *155*
12. The Nature of the Japanese *163*
13. Japanese Originality *177*
14. "This Strange Land" *191*
15. A New Consensus *203*
16. The Gift of Japanese Design *215*

Afterword *231*

Preface

On September 21, 2008, at precisely 1:30 in the afternoon I was standing on a shore of the English Coast. This wasn't the English Coast in Britain, but rather the one in Hanamaki, Iwate Prefecture, in the northeast region of Japan that is called Tohoku. The stretch of white sedimentary rock along the banks of the Kitakami River that winds its way through the town and region was given that name by poet and visionary Miyazawa Kenji. He imagined the white stone face of the embankment to be like the White Cliffs of Dover. Never having left Japan himself, it was only one innocent figment among the many of his colossal imagination.

Why, you may ask, be so specific about the time of day?

It so happens that Kenji drew his last breath at 1:30 pm on September 21 1933, precisely seventy-five years before I found myself standing on the bank of the river. The wind rose and a shudder coursed through my entire body. Was Kenji trying to tell me something? Was his intriguing character Kaze no Matasaburo, the "boy who flew in on the wind," racing through my body?

Kenji's message to his Japanese readers—and later to readers all over the world—was that a single human being can find true happiness and fulfillment in life. This is the message that I have distilled from the work of Japan's greatest poet of the modern era.

Despite the enormous tragedy of the Great East Japan Earthquake and tsunami of March 2011 and the resulting nuclear crisis in Fukushima prefecture, and despite nearly three decades of Japan wandering in a fog of national diffidence since the bursting of the asset bubble in the early 1990s, Japan is still a country of hope and promise.

Today, when people in Japan—young and old, men and women—are searching for insight and guidance into how personal happiness and fulfillment can be attained, Kenji, through his writing and his life, offers at least one solution: Find personal happiness in the happiness of others.

But this can by no means be the sole solution, for to rely on collective altruism may prove an elusive exercise at best. In fact, Japanese people can look to their customs, traditions and unique ways of thinking in order to reshape, reinvent and reimagine the future. The key to the creation of a dynamic future is found in your country's culture. The key to your own future lies in your personal relationship to that culture, either as passive observer or active participant.

That is what this book is about: It is a roadmap for Japanese people toward the future. The nation of Japan is absolutely essential to the world. When Japanese people begin to believe that again, Japan's place in the world will be restored. It will not be restored by aggressive posturing or revanchism, or through the recreation of imagined past glories. Culture does not ride on the crests of an economic and political model that may have served the nation in a previous era. It is the exact opposite. Economics and politics advance on the wave of culture. When Japanese people come to see this again, confidence in the Japanese economy and the nation's positive geopolitical identity will be restored both at home and overseas.

Because of the malaise that has haunted Japan for upwards of thirty years now, an entire generation of young people seems to be lacking in confidence when it comes to building a life for themselves that has true personal value, a life that shows them a way they can contribute to the social well-being of the people of their country. To them, older generations burnt themselves out rebuilding Japan after the war, dedicating body and soul to the company or the small business or the farm. And what did it leave us? Fathers who didn't know their children; women who ceased wanting to give birth; old people feeling abandoned by both family and state.... Naturally young people thought, in a reverse of Kenji's famous incantation: "That is the kind of person/I do *not* want to be."

But then, too, they rightfully ask themselves: What kind of

person should I become? Where is the model for me in this country? Barack Obama may have been a model for American blacks, but he can hardly be a model for a young person born in Japan, where the history, customs and social system are so different from those in the United States. What about Thomas Edison as a model? Or Bill Gates? Or Marie Curie, Helen Keller? These are all figures whose accomplishments are held up to Japan's young people as exemplary. These people may be wonderful role models, but they appeared in different countries, under very different circumstances from those that exist in Japan.

Many young people are deeply pessimistic about Japan's future, as if the current gray landscape will forever stretch all the way to the horizon and beyond. Some of them retreat into their houses and don't go out. The number of *hikikomori* among people in Japan—that is, people who shut themselves in their homes or obsessively avoid all encounters with people other than immediate family—exceeds a million, and may be as high as 1.5 million. The vast majority of these people are under thirty. They are content to live solitary lives where human contact is conducted electronically, by mobile phone, tablet or computer.

But for the people of the early Meiji era (1868-1912) and those of the immediate postwar period, the world looked a lot bleaker than it does to us now. The value system of the Edo period (1603-1868) was shattered by the emergence of Japan from two and a half centuries of national isolation; a whole new elaborate and labyrinthine social edifice had to be constructed, and an entire nation of people had to be taught to navigate its levels and corridors. The same thing may be said for the third decade of the Showa era, which lasted in its entirety from 1926 until 1989. The new value system established during Meiji and based essentially on the model of the modern European nation-state had produced a society bent on national aggrandizement and imperial conquest. By the beginning of the third decade of Showa, with Japan left in ruins as the result of an unrelenting and indiscriminate bombing campaign by the United States, the people were left in a moral void, a void created by two generations of leaders who had betrayed the humanistic values inherent in Japanese culture. That there are leaders of Japan repeating this very mistake of equating the spirit and morale of the Japanese people with the vacuous ideology of the militaristic past constitutes the clear and present danger facing Japan in our day.

Yet, there is another Japan. It is unlike the rapacious and bellicose nation of the 1930s and early 1940s. This "other Japan" can be reimagined, reinvented and pursued until it becomes the new Japanese reality. This other Japan gets limited exposure in the outside world, because it does not suit the aspirations of the ruling classes who, in today's Japan, are reshaping the nation in the image of their prewar forebears.

It is in a bleak age such as the one Japan now finds itself in that the chance to reinvent oneself personally and one's nation collectively most readily presents itself. It is precisely in such an age that new paradigms present themselves to us—in communication, energy and lifestyle values. The new Bill Gateses and Marie Curies and Thomas Edisons of Japan now have a chance to reimagine Japan and create a truly new country, based on the creations—scientific, artistic and social—that this country has given the world in the past.

Now, once again, one can say with conviction to young Japanese people, "The world is your oyster," though sadly, they are as yet unwilling or unable to believe or embrace it. They have lost their faith that Japan can make a difference in the world.

I am very fond of the words of the pioneering Sumitomo entrepreneur Iba Teigo: "The greatest damage done to the positive development of a venture is caused not by the errors of the young but by the domination of the old."

This applies in all fields of endeavor, not only business. Young people should not blame themselves for the country's past mistakes and inertia. They need to find in themselves qualities that the young people of Meiji (before the country forced them into the military and packed them off to countries in Asia and the South Pacific) and those that the young people of the postwar years in

Japan possessed. In Japanese it is *hangyaku no seishin*: the spirit of rebellion.

Each and every young person, whatever their innate abilities may be, has the potential to imagine and to act on the basis of that imagination. Even people who are older—even as old as me—can still reinvent life for themselves. But it requires on all our parts the deepest evaluation of our culture to find those elements that truly suit the tenor of our times. To honor our ancestors we must first reject them. To validate for ourselves what is valuable in their teachings we must choose only those elements in them that we can use for our own ends.

It is for this reason that I wrote this book, so that the people of Japan can say to themselves, as Miyazawa Kenji once vowed to himself in his poem "Strong in the Rain": "That is the kind of person/I want to be."

I wrote the book to encourage Japanese people to have the confidence to add to this: "That is the kind of person I *will* be."

Roger Pulvers
Tokyo
2020

PART ONE

1

THIS IS MY COUNTRY

*Creativity is the ability to invent a new future
out of the raw materials of the past and present.*
—Yosano Akiko

A long journey had taken me to the moment in September 2008 that I found myself standing, like a statue in the wind, on the bank of the Kitakami River in Kenji's hometown of Hanamaki. There was a time when I had never heard of Miyazawa Kenji and Hanamaki, a time when I had not so much as an inkling of where Kyoto or Osaka was located, what sushi tasted like, or how the Japanese language sounded. I was totally ignorant when it came to anything Japanese: a blank slate. Having grown up in the 1950s and '60s, it was not unusual to draw blanks and be ignorant when it came to Japan. This was before Japan's emergence as a superpower known for its innovation and design.

When I arrived at Tokyo International Airport (Haneda Airport) in the late afternoon of September 14, 1967, I was twenty-three and didn't speak the language. I knew no one in the country. There was a war raging in Vietnam, a war that I felt to be unjustified and brutal. In my heart I was ceasing to see myself as an American; but this was still some years before I gave up my American citizenship and became the citizen of another country. In short, I was at sea. (I came to cherish the feeling of being lost or disoriented in a strange city, of forgetting, for a moment, who or where I was.)

I collected my single battered suitcase from the airport conveyor belt—the suitcase that had been with me throughout my travels over the previous three years across Europe and the U.S.—and enquired at the information desk about a cheap hotel. They recommended a hotel in Meguro, and I asked where I could catch the bus.

"Oh, it's too difficult for you to get a bus there. Please take a taxi."

I had only $300 to my name at the time, and this was going to have to last me, as it seemed to me then, for the rest of my life. I reluctantly slid into the back seat of a taxi and showed the driver the name of the hotel.

That taxi ride ended up costing me 1,500 yen, which, even at 360 yen to the dollar, was still a lot of money to me. (After all, this was the era of the poor traveler's essential companion, *Europe on Five Dollars a Day*.) But it ended up being the most significant taxi ride of my life.

As we drove toward the city in the dusky light of early evening, my eyes were glued to the taxi window. I looked with wonder at all the men and women rushing along the streets on their way to restaurants or home or other destination. I marveled at the kaleidoscope of neon lights. I was seized with astonishment by the nighttime city passing before my eyes.

It was as if I was looking into a magic lantern, the kind that people peered into before the age of movies. That taxi window was the glass face of my magic lantern, flicking images in bright succession. And I whispered to myself right then and there—the memory of this is totally clear to me today—"This is my country. I am going to live in this country until I die."

How did I have the chutzpah to claim Japan as my country after being in it for only the better part of one hour? Someone had told me that Japanese people, while being very polite to foreigners, rarely accepted them as part of their ethnic "family." Would I be able to "be a Japanese" without the Japanese people ever accepting me as one? I had come straight out of the American Jewish culture and so was not lacking in a healthy strain of self-confidence, what my relatives in Brooklyn, where I was born, called "noiv." But to arrive in Japan and proclaim myself Japanese for life, that was beyond the pale of mere chutzpah and bordered on the outrageous.

Had I been a Japanese in a previous life? Had I been a catfish swimming on the muddy bottom of a pond somewhere deep in the Japanese countryside? A couple of years later I first heard the name

Lafcadio Hearn, whose Japanese name was Koizumi Yakumo, a man about whose life I subsequently wrote a novel, *The Dream of Lafcadio Hearn*. I felt the need to come to terms with this man and how he assimilated his experiences in Japan. I saw him at first as a kind of template, though, virtually by his own admission, his Japan was an illusion wrapped in a shadow, not much of a template to cling to.

Lafcadio Hearn felt utterly at home in Japan from the very instant he set foot on the Yokohama dock in April 1890, exactly as I had felt in September 1967. Perhaps we were predestined to come to Japan. Or was it sheer accident, just a caprice of coincidences that had led us there? A magazine made the offer to Hearn to go to Japan, where he had never so much as contemplated going; a war in a Southeast Asian country and circumstances that led to my leaving Europe (more on this later) led me to the seat in that Tokyo taxi on a sweltering summer's evening in 1967. Hearn and I didn't choose Japan. We literally just ended up there. I felt the need to come to terms with him. We both immersed ourselves totally in Japan and, dare I say, had one crucial thing in common: We carried little cultural bias and no Western agenda.

A small cage was opened at Lafcadio Hearn's funeral in 1904, setting birds into the air, the soul of the deceased presumably taking flight with them. His coffin was draped in chrysanthemums and fragrant olive, adorned by a laurel wreath. Seven Buddhist priests read the sutras at Kobudera (now Jishoin Enyuji temple) in Shinjuku Ward's Ichigaya-Tomihisacho district in Tokyo, where Hearn had frequently enjoyed strolling among the gravestones.

The nonJapanese community was vehemently put off and insulted by the choice of venue. As if having Buddhist priests officiate wasn't bad enough, they were enraged by the Occidental's profane choice of a temple for the funeral. He himself had been a living outrage to the nonJapanese community, a role that he, as an anti-Christian and anti-imperialist, had thoroughly relished. Only three foreigners attended his funeral.

Forty Japanese professors and about a hundred students from

the two universities at which he had taught—Tokyo Imperial University (now the University of Tokyo) and Waseda University—were, as a matter of courtesy, also in attendance. However, this gives the wrong impression of his popularity among the Japanese population at the time. In his day Lafcadio Hearn was a virtual unknown in his adopted country. It was outside Japan that he was widely admired as the premier and true interpreter of the ways of the Japanese, viewed with curiosity or ruefully by those in the West as far and away the world's most inscrutable people.

In the short period of fourteen years that he had lived in Japan, Hearn felt that he had become privy to the most deeply cherished secrets of the Japanese mindset. His obituary appeared in a host of American newspapers. On November 26, 1904, two months to the day after his death, the *Oregon Journal* wrote of him as the "Poet of Japan—he had become Japanese Thru and Tru [sic], tried to hide himself from foreigners and to bind himself closer and closer to his chosen country." Author and poet Noguchi Yone (father of sculptor Isamu Noguchi) called Hearn "a delicate, easily broken Japanese vase."

The crucial word here is "Japanese," for Lafcadio Hearn, born smack in the middle of the nineteenth century to a Greek mother and an Irish father, had become a Japanese citizen, adopting the name Koizumi Yakumo six years after arriving in the country. In his writings he extolled as unique and exquisite every feature of the old Japanese character and folk culture, cheerfully alienating himself from white Christian society in Japan. He recreated a Japan that was receding into the shadows—for he had always preferred shadows to light—and plunged into them, wallowing in the illusion that *this alone* was the "real" Japan.

This all gave rise to a bizarre and fascinating paradox: As Hearn's fame waned in the West following his death, his reputation rose to great heights in Japan. On September 19, 1904, a week before Hearn's death, Japanese troops under the command of General Nogi Maresuke had attacked the Russians at Port Arthur, the strategic outpost at Lushun Port in China. Hearn would not live to see Japan's victory in the Russo-Japanese War the following year; but that victory set Japan on a course of chauvinistic conquest that pumped adrenalin through veins already streaming with national pride. It was at this point, as Hearn was being increasingly seen in the West as an apologist for the "Oriental upstart"—which he most definitely was not—that the Japanese adopted their not-so-native son as a spokesman. Here it was, written in English by a nonJapanese, proof that the Japanese soul was more profound, subtler and more potent in its pure spirituality than anything the materialistic West could possibly muster. They saw in him someone who had come to Japan without a hidden Western agenda, which was true. They also saw someone who loved Japan unequivocally, which was not true. (Since then they have conveniently ignored his unequivocal and often rigorously anti-Japanese side.)

Hearn had been an orphan of Europe, a rootless cosmopolitan and wanderer seemingly at home nowhere but in Japan. Now he was being brandished by the Japanese, their sharpened sword, as witness to the superiority of their national character over people in Western and other Asian nations.

How did a misfit who failed to find lasting companionship or solace in Europe and the United States come to be a shining symbol for the Japanese of their self-styled superiority?

The odds had been against him all his life.

His parents took him from his mother's homeland in the Ionian Islands of Greece, then a British Army protectorate, to his father's home in Dublin when he was just two years old. It was not an uncommon type of liaison. Charles Bush Hearn, a dashing surgeon in the British Army, had encountered local beauty Rosa Kassimati at a dance. She was illiterate, though of good family. A son was born; and when Rosa was pregnant with their second child, Lafcadio, the couple decided to marry. The first son passed away shortly after Lafcadio's birth on June 27, 1850. Later Charles was able to have the marriage annulled because Rosa had been unable to sign the certificate.

When Lafcadio and his mother reached Dublin in 1852 they

would have seen a city ravaged by destitution and overpopulation at the end of the Great Famine. While Ireland had lost up to a quarter of its population through death and emigration, the population of the capital had swelled. Mother and son were fortunate. They were put under the care of Charles's aunt, Sarah Brenane, a pious martinet living in the well-to-do district of Rathmines. (The house today bears a plaque commemorating Hearn's years there.)

Rosa, who became pregnant once more after a short visit by her husband, abandoned Lafcadio and Dublin in 1854. (Charles re-encountered an old sweetheart, Alicia Crawford, on this visit and eventually married her.) How could a woman born and raised on the Greek isles cope with the gray misery of the Dublin climate and the strict domestic practices of a household whose language she did not understand? Lafcadio was never to see his mother again, and had only brief and deeply unsatisfactory encounters with his father. He never met his younger brother James (who passed away in St. Louis in 1933, twenty-nine years after Lafcadio's death), though both of them, by chance, ended up living in the state of Ohio at the same time. He felt, until he arrived in Japan in 1890, that the fetters of family were something he would not encumber himself with in his wildest dreams.

But it was with just such a family that Hearn found himself fettered late in his life. This Poe-faced outsider and aficionado of the eerie and the bizarre, who any number of times had been bereft of the barest means of subsistence, living off the smell of an oily rag in London, sleeping rough and fossicking in the gutters of the Rue Morgue in Cincinnati and New Orleans for bits of culture to cling to, was eventually to earn a formidable salary as a teacher in Japan while supporting up to eleven people, including his wife, four children, in-laws and servants. What an astonishing turn of events! He published, on average, a book for every year he lived in Japan and was read eagerly not only by Americans for his esoteric insights into Japanese mores, traditions and vansihing lifestyle, but also by readers in China, India and Europe.

After being sent out of his great-aunt's home and packed off, at age nineteen, to the United States, Hearn traveled to Cincinnati, where he landed a job as a reporter at the city's leading newspaper. His output was prodigious. His articles, largely dealing with serious crime, were full of meticulous gruesome detail. They were devoured by readers. However, his marriage to a black woman in June 1874 caused an outrage, and he was sacked from his job. The woman, Alethea Foley, was, like Hearn's mother, illiterate; and, like his parents' marriage, his was not considered valid. Ohio law at the time prohibited interracial marriages.

Hearn left Cincinnati and drifted to New Orleans, where once again he became a popular reporter. After spending two years on Martinique in the West Indies, he returned to the United States, although his prospects for employment were meager. And then Lady Luck smiled on him in the form of an invitation to go to Japan and write up his impressions for *Harper's* magazine. The American public was crying out for information about the country that had emerged from the obscurity of isolation and was intriguing the world with its mysterious culture. Hearn crossed Canada by train, embarked from Vancouver and arrived at Yokohama on April 4, 1890, age thirty-nine.

Through the good offices of Professor Basil Hall Chamberlain of Tokyo Imperial University, he was offered a job teaching at a middle school in the old castle town of Matsue on the coast of the Sea of Japan. There he met Koizumi Setsu, nearly eighteen years his junior. Setsu had been married and divorced, which made her highly ineligible for another union to a Japanese man. Of course, no one would have imagined that an eligible foreigner would come to live in Matsue. But such an eccentric one did; and in January 1891, the two were married.

The Hearns moved to Kumamoto in Kyushu, where for three years Lafcadio developed a particular contempt for the city, writing, "[Kumamoto is] my realization of a prison in the bottom of hell." Then they moved to Kobe, where once again he practiced his old profession of journalism. Severe eyesight problems prevented him from continuing, and before long he found himself on the teacher's podium at Tokyo Imperial University. He longed to leave Japan, but illness and lack of opportunity prevented it.

Hearn became known again in the West after the Second World War, when Americans in particular craved colorful information and exotic detail about their new friends in the Far East. As Japanese culture coursed ever further from the vanishing world that he had depicted, Hearn's idealized and adulatory image of the country suited Japanese needs once again, this time to reassure them that they had the spiritual backbone to withstand the heavy weight of American "values" lowered, willy-nilly, on their shoulders.

Hearn may have been a story "reteller" of great charm and perspicacity, but his prose is weighed down by the florid clichés of the Victorian era and its stilted lyricism. It is fortunate for his reputation among the Japanese that this flowery language translates well into Japanese. His true genius, however, lies in the brilliant clarity and careful detail of his reportage. He is, I believe, one of the foremost ethnographic documentarians of American life in the second half of the nineteenth century.

If you want to experience his best writing, read the hundreds of articles he wrote about American subculture during his years in the country. He does not shirk from any detail, however morbid or distasteful. He has no time for the decoy that is decorum. He does accurate fieldwork like a present-day anthropologist. He not only visits but throws himself into places where others fear to go: the morgues, the dens of crime, the slaughterhouses, the dangerous haunts of every pariah on every skid row in town, always with an empathetic outlook on the misery of the people and animals caught up there. He writes with great sympathy about all aspects of black culture, from the argot of the roustabouts on the Cincinnati docks to the practitioners of Creole folk medicine in New Orleans ("for tetanus, cockroach tea is given; a poultice of boiled cockroaches is placed over the wound"). There was not a drop of racist blood in Hearn's body. In the era of post-bellum America, where white brutality against blacks was vicious, arbitrary and unrelenting, Hearn embraced and extolled black subculture.

As a journalist, Hearn had an indefatigable curiosity and an equally indefatigable amount of sheer nerve. In May 1876 he asked to be hoisted up the spire of Cincinnati's tallest structure, the Cathedral of St. Peter-in-Chains, and described the city from there though petrified with fear. He later wrote to his friend, the musicologist Henry Krehbiel, of the intense delight he felt "piddling on the universe."

Had he lived another two or three decades, he would have been appalled at the manner in which the self-aggrandizing powerbrokers in the cultural establishment of Japan used him to justify incursions into Asia. He loathed the modern Japanese male and what he stood for, and in this he recognized the futility of his task, a futility keenly felt toward the end of his years, when he heard "nothing but soldiers and the noise of bugles." He worshipped the static and wanted to see his beloved quaint Japan remain as sweet as it always was in his mind's eye and in the eyes of the world, bemoaning all progress: "What, what can come out of all this artificial fluidity!"

He was the shadow-maker, the illusionist who conjured up his own visions of Japan and gladly lost himself in them. But toward the end of his life, he seriously considered leaving Japan and returning to the United States. Perhaps he realized that it was there that he had created his most accomplished work, attaining something he savored: notoriety. Again an irony emerges. He is remembered now in United States, if at all, not for his superb reportage on nineteenth-century America but for his adoration of a long-gone Japan.

There was a chance to get back to America when Jacob Gould Schurman, president of Cornell University, agreed at the end of 1902 to invite Hearn to present a series of lectures. The proposal never materialized into an invitation. This may have been due to an outbreak of typhoid fever on campus, causing him to be wary of visitors from Asia, although it is much more likely that Schurman was more wary of Hearn's notorious cantankerousness than of unwanted Eastern maladies. At any rate, the proposal was withdrawn in March 1903.

The cruelties of Hearn's childhood had made him painfully shy of any lasting relationship. Yet he was uncannily caring toward his eldest son, Kazuo, and of his wife, Setsu, whom he called "Lovely Little Mama Sama," writing to her from the seaside just a month before he died: "I feel lonely sometimes; I wish I could see your sweet face. I beseech you that you will take care of your own self. … You must never think of any danger which might occur to your boy." He signed those letters with his Japanese name, Koizumi Yakumo, also known as Lafcadio Hearn, is buried beside Setsu and Kazuo in the Zoshigaya Cemetery in Tokyo.

I discuss Hearn here in such detail because of the legacy he left us: that whether through prolonged study of the Japanese language and culture, which Hearn did not have the benefit of, or the insight of objectively scrutinized personal experience, a person writing about Japan must pursue authenticity above all. In virtually all cases, popular books about Japan written by foreigners present a portrait of the people and their country that their readers may find attractive and incisive but that lack a sense of reality for the Japanese.

Lafcadio Hearn was the first nonJapanese to forge a double-edged sword that shone with authenticity for both Japanese and nonJapanese, though sadly for him the two views of him were not held simultaneously. The goal of a person wishing to write about Japanese culture and life today should be to inform both sides with equal depth and insight.

I had never heard the name Lafcadio Hearn when I arrived in Japan in 1967, and I knew even less Japanese than he did when he arrived seventy-seven years previous to that. I was a tabula rasa aching to be covered in script.

When I stepped out of the taxi from the airport that first day in Japan, the driver rushed to the trunk of the car, pulled out my old suitcase and put it on the sidewalk. I paid him 1,500 yen and he bowed his head, saying, *sumimasen*. Once in my room, I took my pocket dictionary from my suitcase and looked up sumimasen.

The definition given was "Excuse me." Why, I wondered, would a taxi driver say "excuse me" when being given the money that was coming to him? It wasn't long before I learned that sumimasen also meant "thank you." This taught me an even more valuable lesson: Rely primarily on life experiences for the understanding of foreign languages, not dictionaries.

That night in 1967 set my life on a path that I am still on, on a journey of self-discovery via Japan and its culture, a journey that is still in progress with the same unaltered wonder that I had when staring with astonishment into my magic lantern. The lights in the first glimpses into the magic lantern of "my" country and the wind that went through me on the bank of the Kitakami River are the two decisive elements that have defined time for me, a frame—of light and wind—in the picture that became my life.

Before coming to Japan, I had never eaten a Japanese meal. There were Japanese restaurants in Los Angeles, where I grew up, but most of them were in Little Tokyo or neighborhoods where Japanese Americans lived, both of which were far from our home. I couldn't name a single famous Japanese. I hadn't read a Japanese novel. I had seen only two Japanese movies: *Godzilla*, which, because it was dubbed, I mistook for an American film; and *Woman in the Dunes*. (How could I know, when I saw *Woman in the Dunes* in 1964, that twenty years later I would be directing its star, Kishida Kyoko, on stage in Tokyo?)

I bring all of this up not only to expose my ignorance of Japan at the time, but to show how limited the impact of Japanese culture on the United States was in the 1950s and '60s. You could get authentic Japanese food in Little Tokyo, which was located in downtown L.A., and Japanese films did show in the city, in particular at one cinema, the La Brea Theater, which had been opened by the Japanese film production company Toho to highlight their films. But eating Japanese food and seeing Japanese movies were strictly minority interests for Americans. Nobody I knew ever went to see a Japanese movie (except *Godzilla*) or ventured downtown to Little Tokyo to eat what was then considered a very exotic cuisine.

There were a few Japanese American kids at Alexander Hamilton High School, but they were generally shy and kept to themselves. Japanese people lived in homes clustered in and around certain outer Los Angeles suburbs and were by and large content with their quiet and unobtrusive middle-class lives. It was a general feature of Japanese American life to keep a low profile, to gain the respect of the majority by being inconspicuous.

I was twenty-one when I had my first conversation with a Japanese person. It was on a train from Moscow to Leningrad in the summer of 1965. He was, like me, a student traveling alone, very neatly dressed in a check shirt, khaki pants and slick shoes. He didn't speak English or Russian, and of course I spoke no Japanese.

He reached into his shirt pocket, took out a blue and white packet of Hi-Lite cigarettes and offered me one. I smiled, declining the cigarette, as he lit up with the flash of a Zippo lighter.

"Japanese?" I asked, pointing at the cigarette.

"Yes, Japanese!" he said, baring his teeth and emitting a huge puff of smoke that lingered around his mouth.

That was the extent of our conversation, I'm afraid. I didn't learn anything about Japan, but I do recall being very surprised that the Japanese had their own brand of cigarettes.

A few months prior to that, a young Japanese couple had approached me as I was crossing Harvard Yard on the Harvard campus. They pointed to me and their camera, saying, "Picture, okay?"

So, if any Japanese person reading this book has seen a photo taken by their parents (or grandparents) at Harvard in the spring of 1965 of a gawky student wearing Bermuda shorts and white socks, and holding a big Russian dictionary with a navy-blue cover—the dreaded Soviet dictionary by Sergei Ozhegov that Vladimir Nabokov deprecatingly called "the blue dragon"—I would appreciate being contacted via the publisher of this book.

The single incident that led me, albeit circuitously, to Japan in September 1967 occurred nearly ten years previous to that time, in mid-October 1957. It is an incident that is entirely unrelated to

Japan. Yet as my life transpired, it turned out to be the basis for my eventual presence in Japan. This is how things in life happen. One thing leads to another, leapfrogging over what should be a rational progression of events, and then, all of a sudden, you are somewhere else, encountering entirely different people. Dust is wiped from the pocked kitchen table, and the colored textures on walls you once knew change forever. The faces of friends fade from your life; and suddenly you are another person inhabiting your own skin. And this is all for the better.

That single incident was the launch by the Soviet Union of the first artificial satellite, Sputnik (which means "traveling companion" in Russian) on October 4, 1957. This was by far the most exciting event of my childhood, exceeding even the day of my Bar Mitzvah when I no longer had to go to Hebrew School and endure the platitudes presented there as wisdom.

The successful launch of Sputnik created a shock wave that hit my country like a tsunami. How could a communist country like the Soviet Union, and a "country of atheists" to boot, achieve something that the United States of America had only dreamt of? It was unthinkable. America immediately launched into a space program of its own and started to pour immense sums of money into science education. Capitalist ideology had blinded Americans to the truth that any country was capable of great scientific achievements if their people put their mind to it, even "backward" Russians who presumably didn't believe in God.

To me there was a profound lesson in Sputnik, even then. Age thirteen, I wasted no time at all in taking out my telescope at night and watching the artificial satellite streak across the sky over my Los Angeles home for the three weeks it remained in space. It may be hard for young people today to imagine how shocking this was to us. A manmade instrument was put into orbit and circling the Earth in about ninety minutes, and it was flying right over my house! My imagination sprouted powerful wings and flew up to and alongside it through the heavens. I became Sputnik's sputnik.

I dragged my dad outside at night so that he could see it too. Dad was unimpressed.

"Well, what is it? Just a lump of metal flying through the sky. You get back inside and do your homework."

I could not understand why he wasn't thrilled to death by the sight of Sputnik right there over our heads.

We had my grandmother's old radio in the garage. It was one of those bulky prewar pieces of furniture that once held pride of place in the home. Families used to sit around them at night and listen together in the yellow light of the living room, an iconic scene out of a painting by Norman Rockwell.

Grandma's radio, which was soon to be in the hands of the rubbish collector, had not been switched on in years. I plugged it in and it started to hum, emitting static. I turned the huge dial to the frequency that had been published in the *Los Angeles Mirror*, and lo and behold, I heard the beep-beep-beep of Sputnik as it was flying overhead. Now this little miracle of scientific achievement was speaking directly to me, a thirteen-year-old boy in L.A. in awe of a manmade object that could orbit the Earth.

The very next day I went to the local library, borrowed a book on elementary Russian and started to teach myself the Cyrillic alphabet. My parents were seriously worried. I could hear them whispering in the next room about how they could possibly get me "back on the right track."

Dad remarked to mother, "I never should have bought him that damn telescope!"

I quickly took my telescope lenses off the shelf and shoved them under my bed. If they took away my telescope, I would ... well, I would just probably cry my eyes out and keep gazing at the stars with the naked eye. While there was already a smog problem in Los Angeles in the 1950s, you could still see the Milky Way on clear nights, and you could always look up with wonder at "your traveling companion" as it sailed in its orbit around this planet and came right back again ninety minutes later.

It wasn't until four years from that time, when I enrolled at UCLA in 1961, that I was able to study Russian in a proper way. In the end, I took only two years of Russian in the three years I spent as an undergraduate. (I completed a four-year university course in three years, and then finished a two-year master's course in one year; so I had just turned twenty-one when I left Harvard with the MA.)

Upon graduation from UCLA in June 1964 I could read simple Russian, but just like so many Japanese students of English, I didn't understand what native speakers were saying to me, and I certainly was unable to get out any more than a few phrases of simple greeting myself.

I have told this to my Japanese students over the years. On my twentieth birthday, I spoke only English. If you had met me then and asked me, "Are you someone who can speak foreign languages?" I would definitely have answered, "No way. I have no talent for that sort of thing."

After my first visit to the Soviet Union in the summer of 1964, I was able to speak Russian fluently and read it almost as easily as English. My time at Warsaw University in 1966-67 afforded me the ability to speak, read and write Polish. And within about six months of arriving in Japan in 1967, I was able to speak Japanese, though the ability to read and write the language came much later. And so, between ages twenty and twenty-four I had managed to master three foreign languages, and rather difficult ones at that.

This no doubt appears as if I am sounding my own horn, but I assure you that I am not writing this here to brag about a talent for languages. If we have abilities, we should not be shy in acknowledging them, just as it is never wise to claim some knowledge or ability for yourself that you do not have. Never claim that you can speak a language when you know only a few dozen words and phrases. One day someone is going to speak that language to you and the cat will be out of the bag.

This is what I have told my students over the years. When you are young, your brain is like a sponge. You can absorb anything you wish. All you need is curiosity and passion. I had both of these, thanks, in the first instance, to my little traveling companion in the sky. And I found an ability in myself that I never knew I had.

Speaking a foreign language allows you to be yourself and someone else at the same time; it allows you to view yourself objectively, to use your imagination in saying things, sometimes very trite and mundane things, in a novel way. It allows you to get under the skin of the people you are talking to, to think what they think, to see what they see, to feel what they feel. There is no doubt in my mind that the study of foreign languages is the most revealing, enlightening and exciting thing I have ever done in my life. Without it, I would not be the person I am today. I might have been a businessman, a lawyer or a doctor. But I know that I wouldn't have been myself.

I discovered in 1957, at the tender age of thirteen, when I told my parents that I wanted to be an astronomer and started an argument with them that lasted for several decades, that the dream they were dreaming for my life was not my own. It was theirs. Dad wanted me to be what he had not become, what he had dreamed of for himself but had not been able to achieve: a respectable Jewish profession (in order, doctor, lawyer, certified public accountant) … and wealth.

In actuality, every generation has its own dream or dreams, and that's how it should be. Yet the one thing that young people in any country and any era should be wary of is taking on the burden of the unfulfilled dreams of the previous generation.

To see how this applies to present-day Japan, let's look back to the two great eras of progressive transformation in this country. This may tell us what is lacking in the present era, why young people today are trapped in a very undreamlike quagmire left them by their elders.

The Japanese people of the Meiji era had a dream: to absorb global values of education and development in order to create a modern nation-state that could stand shoulder to shoulder with the dominant states of the West. They rejected the isolationist principles of the previous two and a half centuries. Their individual pride derived from the achievements of the collective, be it their village, town or city, or their country. The leaders of Meiji Japan were young and keen on reinventing what it meant to be Japanese in the modern world.

The second great era of transformation came after the Second World War, when virtually every major and most minor cities had been reduced to rubble. Again, young men and women felt betrayed by their past. They were bitter about having been indoctrinated in school with a militaristic and chauvinist mindset. They rejected the past and created a new ethos that allowed for individual achievement in culture and commerce. Their pride came from their conviction that Japan could be reconceived as a robust, peaceful and creative force in the world.

In other words, the people of Meiji and of postwar Japan followed *their own* dreams. And the leitmotiv of these dreams was rebellion. They implicitly understood what poet Yosano Akiko was telling them in the words quoted at the top of this chapter, namely that the raw materials for a nation's reinvention exist in its own culture, and that the theme had to be creative reinvention, not reverent continuation.

By the 1960s, when the postwar generation of writers, playwrights, filmmakers, graphic artists, photographers, designers and other creative people was coming into its own, the media, particularly the print media, was awash in lively polemical debates; little theaters were proliferating and booming, mounting productions of plays that questioned fundamental notions underpinning Japanese society; filmmakers attacked every stultifying aspect of Japanese social life, past and present; and thousands of ordinary people joined students in demonstrations against what they saw as a new acceptance of militarism in the guise of strategic cooperation with the United States.

There was even a fascinating variation on the postwar generation's aspiration toward an independent and open Japan in the 1980s, when the so-called *shinjinrui*, or "new species," debunked the overly serious messages of their elders and created a "Japan Lite" brand of playful merchandise and self-indulgent fun. This spirit translated easily into the video game and anime booms that were to follow. This too was a kind of rebellion against a past that had required Japanese people to be the "Three D's": diligent, disciplined and dour.

But what of the present? Aren't today's young urged to follow a dream? Yes, they are. But it is a dream that can no longer provide pride, either collective or individual, for them as the new generation of Japanese. This new dream, concocted by the older generation that had failed to lay the road for progress in a new direction, is devoid of the spirit of rebellion. This road leads them backward, back to the "good old days" when Japanese kept their noses to the grindstone and their heads bowed humbly low in the face of authority. The road sign reads: "Put up with austerity and buckle down."

Where is their spirit of rebellion, their hard cold eye on the vagaries of the past? After all, the previous generations have only succeeded in plunging Japan into a thirty-year-long period of stagnation. The seniority system in business and government today is a euphemism for the institutionalization of stodgy and repressive inaction dominated by males. New policies are largely very old items repackaged. As for new ideas, they are coming from NPOs and citizen groups in the smaller cities and towns and from venture businesses begun, against all odds in Japan, by bold newcomers. People's expectations of social innovation emerging from Tokyo are at the lowest ebb in the past half century.

The medium of the internet and its use in social networking might have given young people the tools they need to take the dissemination of information into their own hands. But young Japanese are unlike young people in many other countries around the world who use these exciting media to invent their own take on their societies. Instead, Japanese have taken the new technology as an excuse to withdraw further into themselves or their own world of "private little happinesses."

Pride in the nation today is surely expressed when a Japanese soccer team or athlete scores a momentous victory against foreign teams or individuals, or when a Japanese film or actor wins an Oscar. But such pride is outwardly generated. It depends on recognition awarded Japan or Japanese people by the foreign world. It is not primarily an inherent pride.

What is lacking is a spirit of heresy and dissent, the gut feeling that you have somehow been misled by your parents' and grandparents' generations and that you must muster your own sense of pride on the basis of values which you yourself create, in the first instance, for your peers.

You cannot pass on an outdated version of a dream. Education should give children the tools to rebel and the means to dream their own dreams. Knowledge that simply rehashes the past is useless. Knowledge that does not give people the abilities to predict the future is equally useless.

In that sense, we have failed the young generation by not doing this, by trying to pawn off our own stale dreams of a "once great Japan" to them—"great" in Meiji imperial terms or "great" in late Showa rapid-growth terms. The three decades of the Heisei era, now over, saw an entire nation running in place. Very little was accomplished politically or economically; very little culture of lasting value was created. Thank goodness that this is all behind us now … or is it?

I, for one, am waiting patiently for the time when young Japanese realize our failure and act on that realization in their own fashion and on their own terms. Until then they will be plagued by the realization that they have somehow disappointed the nation by not "living up to" the past.

With me it all began with Sputnik. I have the Soviet rocket scientists to thank for my own dream and for the way my life turned out. If it hadn't been for Sputnik, I would not have studied Russian. If I had not gone to the Soviet Union, I wouldn't have gone later to Poland, to see a different communist country and to view the Soviet Union from the standpoint of one of its neighbors. If I hadn't had to leave Poland suddenly when I was swept up in a huge international spy scandal, I wouldn't have returned so quickly to the United States, where I was in danger of being drafted and sent to fight in Vietnam. If I hadn't decided to leave my country for good rather than kill innocent people in an unjust war to defend what American leaders called "the free world," I would never have gone to Japan.

It is not only novelists who create lives for their fictional characters by linking coincidences, treating time as if it proceeds like a grasshopper leaping through a field. Life doesn't unfold with seamless logic. It proceeds in directionless leaps and unpredicted bounds. The direction taken often becomes clear only after some considerable distance is covered.

Everyone knows the proverb "Look before you leap." The Japanese equivalent is *ishibashi o tataite wataru*. "Knock on the stone bridge before you cross it." I'm afraid that I have never been good at knocking on things before rushing across them. I just leap across the bridge in big jumps, perhaps too afraid to so much as glance downward, keeping my sight on the night sky as I rush into the unknown.

I am still dashing ahead on the bridge with my eyes fixed on the stars.

2

THE PUZZLE COMES TOGETHER TO FORM A PICTURE

Ask most people anywhere in the world now at the beginning of the new Reiwa era, "How would you characterize the Japanese people and nation?" and the common answer would in all probability be something like this: "They are polite, diligent and quirky, but dour. They lack a sophisticated sense of humor. They are largely a nation of conformists who prefer doing the same thing and acting the same way. They are resilient, but stiff and formal. Japanese culture is great, but it is culturally homogeneous. There is little true ethnic variety. Japan used to be an innovative country, but now its people are sorely lacking in originality and energy. If there were no Japan, little in the world would be different."

Well, it's all pretty negative and pessimistic. There seems to be almost no good news coming out of Japan today. In fact, while all Japanese people might not agree with the above description, many today would share its negativism and pessimism.

I have passed my fiftieth year in Japan, and I have never found the country so deep in a psychological depression. The perfect term to describe this state of the individuals and the nation of Japan is "the doldrums."

The doldrums is originally a term of the sea, describing that part of the ocean where the winds from the northern and southern hemispheres converge, leading to a state of stagnant calm. Yes, that seems to characterize Japan today. Stagnant calm. Except that the winds battering Japan are coming now not from the north and south but from the West and the East.

Despite the above description, I have come to see Japan and the Japanese in an entirely different way. To me, the Japanese are not dour, but exceedingly good natured. Not morose and glum (most of the time), but pleasant and bright, with a sophisticated and fun-loving sense of humor. Not quirky, but individualistic.

To me, they are not rigid but adaptable in virtually any circumstance. This is not a nation of conformists, but merely people who act in conventional ways in public. In private—which is the only true test of a people—they can be utterly eccentric and downright whacky. Japanese culture, in actuality, is rich in variety in any aspect you wish to consider.

This is most certainly a country of immense originality. And as for energy, yes, it is true that Japanese people lack energy today. Three words borrowed from English that used to apply to the Japanese are now, alas, obsolescent. They are *fuaito* (fight, meaning "dogged determination"), *hassuru* (hustle) and *hangurii* (hungry, in the context of ambition). But, a nation's energy is a thing that is never lost, only put aside and conserved. Just look at China, India, Indonesia and Poland. It was only a matter of time before the cultures of those countries provided the vehicle to propel them ahead. Someday, and I think rather soon, too, Japanese people will once again be displaying and expending the kind of energy they did in the two earlier "Eras of Great Transformation," namely the Meiji and early Taisho eras, and the three decades following the end of the Second World War.

I am positive and optimistic about Japan. The world of the twenty-first century would be a very different place if there were no Japan. The world needs Japan even more today than it did when Japan was considered a "great" country by people around the world. I truly believe that customs and ways of thinking originating in Japan can be of great service to the contemporary world, even save many countries from serious problems that could destroy their peace, stability and happiness.

But each and every Japanese person has to understand what it is about Japanese life and culture that is of universal value to the world, how to acquire that understanding and communicate it globally. The Japanese motto of this century should be not "the isolating uniqueness of Japanese culture" but "the broad universality of Japanese culture."

It wasn't until a few years into this century that I came to consider what the world would be like if there were no Japan. No sushi? No karaoke? No, if there were no Japan, I don't mean that young and upwardly mobile salarymen in Sydney would never know the joy of suddenly inhaling deeply through their nostrils in order to ease the sharp shock of wasabi; or that people of newly-acquired wealth in Shanghai would simply have to go to a restaurant and talk to each other because there would be no karaoke bars. Certainly, aspects of Japanese culture like sushi and karaoke that have taken the world by storm would arguably not have existed had there been no Japan to create them. But these are hardly indispensable features of a society. And they are so much a part of life outside Japan that many people no longer associate them exclusively with the country.

I'm thinking, rather, about something much more profound and longer lasting: the very character of the Japanese people and their culture. It dawned on me around the turn of the century that Japan had an enormous contribution to make to the world in the twenty-first century, and not only in what I call "the MASK Phenomenon," MASK standing for: Manga, Anime, Sushi and Karaoke.

Japanese culture in the very broadest sense—encompassing people's behaviors, attitudes, relationships, ways of thinking and modes of imagining and fashioning the world around them—can provide concrete answers to the world's problems in the twenty-first century.

But before I tell you my views on that culture, I feel it necessary to explain to you how I came to feel that way, for it took decades for me to get there. If you do not know the person who is speaking to you, their words and ideas, however potentially attractive, lose persuasiveness. My ideas about Japan and Japanese life are not conceptual rationalizations on the theme of comparative cultures. They come directly out of the most personal encounters.

One's life is lived, of course, as a chronology of events, most of them of such petty significance that they are forgotten moments after they occur. But when reimagining one's life while looking back at it, the chronology itself becomes almost irrelevant. This is because you now know how things have turned out, and you inevitably reorder your life not by the timepiece of sequential events but by the lines, colors and shapes of their themes. One's life becomes a jigsaw puzzle that is put together by matching lines and colors, until, somehow, it all makes sense as a complete picture.

You journey through your life on what is usually a very bumpy road with any number of dangerous potholes. You do not know, most of the time, where this road is going to lead you, so how can you know what has been most important to you in your life up till then? In my case, the road led to Japan. I have dedicated my life to the study of this country and to creating a Japanese life for myself. Everything that happened before I arrived in Japan has to be viewed in light of that.

When I first visited the Soviet Union in 1964, the Second World War had ended a mere nineteen years earlier. To the people of a country that lost 25 million citizens, more than all other countries' losses combined, the memories of war were still fresh. I had been taught in school that we Americans were the ones who conquered Nazi Germany and liberated Europe, unaware of the decisive role of the Red Army. Yet all in all, 70 percent of all the German soldiers who died in the Second World War are today buried within the borders of the old Soviet Union.

I had also been taught that Russians were belligerent communists who despised Americans and, to use a phrase bandied about in later years, "hated our freedoms." And yet, in traveling from Moscow to Pyatigorsk (the town in the Northern Caucasus where the great poet Mikhail Lermontov was killed in a duel in 1841), Kiev, Kharkov (now Khariv), Yalta (the site of the Yalta Conference in February 1945), Sochi (the site of the Winter Olympics in 2014), Riga, Novgorod (the town with one of the oldest churches in Russia) and Leningrad (now St. Petersburg), I found an exceedingly friendly and open people who were as curious about the world as I was. They wanted to learn as much as they could about life in the

United States. I was only sorry that I couldn't answer a question posed to me by a "representative of Soviet youth" who was in his late forties: "How many bricks are there in the Empire State Building?" I told the "young" man more than twice my age that I didn't think the Empire State Building had any bricks in it at all. He squinted suspiciously at me, no doubt convinced that I was being evasive about a piece of information that would have been akin to a state secret had it applied to a structure, such as the Kremlin Wall, in the USSR.

I returned in the summer of 1965 to travel once again around the Soviet Union for a month. Again I was treated with genuine hospitality. But I saw in every town how fearful most Soviet citizens were of their government, which kept a close surveillance over their lives. I felt that I needed another perspective on the Soviet Union, one that was neither Soviet nor American.

In 1966 I applied for a postgraduate scholarship from the National Student Association of the United States. The NSA had an annual exchange program with their Polish equivalent, the Polish Student Association (or ZSP in Polish), and I was fortunate to be chosen as the representative for the academic year 1966-67.

I studied some Polish before leaving and arrived in Warsaw in September 1966 eager to learn how the people in a communist country other than the Soviet Union lived. I loved Poland from the very beginning, spending much more time at Warsaw's inspiring theaters and cinemas than at my seminars in the university. It was in Poland that I first discovered the wonders of theater, and I credit my becoming a playwright and director to the time I spent there.

This all was brought to a crashing halt in the first week of February 1967 by an incident that changed the course of my life forever (and led me, eventually, to Japan).

It turned out that the NSA, despite its having the appearances of a liberal and antiwar organization, was a front for the CIA, which had been funding its activities since 1952 to the tune of up to $400,000 a year. *Ramparts*, a liberal American magazine, was about to publish an article exposing this secret and illegal funding when I received a call at my little Krakow flat from the president of the NSA in Washington. (I had moved to Krakow in January 1967 to study there.)

"I want you to come to London right away. I've bought a plane ticket for you with my credit card."

"Okay," I said, "but why?"

"We need to have a meeting with you."

The thing that shocked me the most about the call was not being "summoned" to London. It was that someone who was still a student, essentially my age, had a credit card. In those days not even my parents possessed a credit card. Back then only the rich had them.

When I arrived in London on Sunday, February 12, 1967, I was taken to the U.S. Embassy at Grosvenor Square and was told by an official there—no doubt one of the embassy's CIA officers—about the *Ramparts* magazine article soon to come out.

"I'll go back to Poland now so everyone will know I am not a spy," I said, in all shocking innocence.

"No. You can't do that. Why don't you go to visit your girlfriend in Paris?" said the official.

"How do you know about her?"

"Never mind. Just stay out of Poland."

"But what about all my clothes and books and stuff?"

"Forget about that. Just stay out of Poland!" he said gruffly, shaking his head and wagging a finger at me.

Out on the street I looked up at the deserted embassy. I felt as if the floor had dropped from below my feet. I was totally bereft.

When the *Ramparts* article came out, it created a scandal that rocked the administration of President Lyndon Johnson. Every major newspaper in the country took up the story. And the focus of press and media attention turned to me. I was on the front page, with photo, of the *Los Angeles Times*. My parents were interviewed on primetime evening news programs. (Dad said, "My son does not work for the CIA. But the CIA is not a dirty word with me!" My mother assured the members of the press that "my son is a normal

American. He likes sports and girls.")

"What was this American student, who speaks Russian and Polish, really doing in Poland? Why did he leave Poland so abruptly? Where is he now?" This is what the media wanted to know.

The CIA, through the journalists who were in their pay or sway and did their bidding when called upon to do so, had tossed me into the invisible cage that is the limelight in order to keep the real CIA informants, my student "buddies" in the NSA, safely out of it.

I did go to France to be with my girlfriend; and it was in a Paris café that I read in *Le Monde* that "Roger Pulvers, suspected CIA spy, is presently in Washington D.C. being debriefed."

Hold on. I'm not in Washington D.C. I'm here in Paris. I'm not a spy.... At least I don't think I'm a spy. Maybe I am and I just don't know it. Maybe I'm not Roger Pulvers. After all, the newspaper says I'm not here.

These thoughts actually occurred to me in my very fragile mental state. I was being presented with a sharp curve in the road and I hadn't a clue as to what lay beyond it. I wasn't sure either whether I could manage to steer myself clear into the future. I was at sea and didn't have anything to cling to in order to stay afloat.

My fragile mental state was exacerbated by the fact that my girlfriend—a young woman I was in love with and wanted to marry—left me for a brilliant young philosophy student. I was crushed, and wept in the shadow of the old church in Villiers-sur-Morin, the village outside Paris where she lived.

I couldn't stay in France for reasons of lost love, and I couldn't go back to Poland where I might have been arrested and thrown in jail. Innocence, in either case, was no advantage. So I returned reluctantly to the United States in May 1967, flying nonstop twelve hours and five minutes from Paris to Los Angeles, for me a psychological leap from one world into another.

It was then that I realized I could no longer stay in the United States. I didn't feel, in my bones, that I was an American any longer, but I didn't know what else I could be either. I was only twenty-three. Everything that I had built up for myself in the world of Russian and Polish studies seemed irrelevant. If I could never return to those countries, what good would it do to continue studying them?

If I stayed in America, I would soon be drafted into a war that I hated more than anything. So I decided to go to Japan. I was not "intrigued by the beauty of the Orient" or "captivated by the charms of Japan," as so many writers and travelers had been in the past. Like Lafcadio Hearn, I knew almost nothing about the country and went there for no particular reason. No, well, at least Hearn had a reason. He had been asked to write about Japan for *Harper's* magazine. I would have to discover what the reason was after my arrival.

I had always loved the feeling of being alone and lost in a city. You walk somewhere and you don't know where you are. You are anonymous. You know no one who passes you by. No one takes the least notice of you. If you were to disappear from the face of the Earth that instant, no one there would care. Perhaps this feeling of savoring disorientation is unusual in people. But I welcome it ... well, so long as it doesn't last overly long.

I would be thrust into the midst of a people where I would have to fend for myself, learn the language, meet people, make a life for myself. Fortunately I had received from an acquaintance the name and telephone number of a Japanese professor. The professor was Wakaizumi Kei. (I write about my dear old friend Wakaizumi Kei in the next chapter.)

Professor Wakaizumi was kind to me from the very first moments of our encounter, and said that there might be a teaching position at the university where he taught, Kyoto Sangyo University. Sandai, as it was called, was a young university, founded in 1965, and both Russian and Polish were taught there, which was exceedingly rare at the time in Japan.

Professor Wakaizumi took me down to Kyoto on the shinkansen at the end of September 1967. In those days there was a standing bar on the shinkansen, with young women tending it. As I stood at the bar, speeding at over 100 miles an hour toward Kyoto, I was elated.

THE PUZZLE COMES TOGETHER

Only a few months before I had felt totally lost, with nowhere to go. Now I wanted more than anything else to be able to stay in Japan and build a new life for myself here.

The president of Kyoto Sangyo University, Araki Toshima, offered me a position as a tenured lecturer teaching Russian and Polish. I was stunned when I learned that President Araki was one of Japan's greatest astronomers, a man who had attended lectures given by Albert Einstein and who had himself taught Japan's two most eminent physicists, Yukawa Hideki and Tomonaga Shin'ichiro. (Much later, I was to have a coincidental brush with Yukawa Hideki's life. See page 134.) President Araki's last words to me at that first encounter were, "Now you're going to have to learn Japanese."

I returned to Tokyo on top of the world. The stars were looking favorably down on me. I wrote my parents that I had found a steady job and was going to settle in Japan. They greeted this news with a bitter resignation. Once again the prodigal son was wandering the world, but in search of what? What dream? Where was this all leading? What was my goal?

Needless to say, when confronted by such questions, I could only keep my lips clamped shut and cock my head in puzzlement. I had no more idea of where my dream was leading me than they did. But I was happy in the moment. Wasn't that enough? (For me it was; for my traditional Jewish parents, of course it wasn't.)

My problem now was a visa. The university had prepared all the necessary papers, including the official offer of work, but the government did not allow you to change your tourist visa into a teaching visa while remaining in Japan. You had to go to another country and wait for the papers to be processed, which took a minimum of four weeks.

"Go back to America and wait there," said a government official to me.

I was in a pickle. I couldn't go back to America. For one thing, it might have been a detour directly to Vietnam. For another, my parents would make life very difficult for me and try to prevent me from returning to Japan. My problem was made worse by the fact that I had less than $200 to my name.

So I went to the nearest country that I could go to: Korea. The plane ticket was cheap, and I knew I could live there on only a few dollars a day.

Choosing Korea was the right decision in more ways than one. I lived in a very cheap inn in the center of the Seoul. I can't remember how much I paid per day, but it was not much more than a dollar for a little room with an *ondol* floor for heating and two meals a day. I had never eaten so many different kinds of pickles in my life, especially for breakfast.

But the best thing about the pension was the eighty-five-year-old proprietor who had a gentle manner and a white wispy beard. I couldn't speak a word of Korean, and he spoke no English. On the first day I said to him …

"*Sumimasen. Nihongo o hanashite kudasai.*" (Excuse me. Please speak Japanese.)

The old proprietor's delicate jaw dropped and he stared at me in total bewilderment. I bowed my head, adding, "*Sumimasen. Boku nihongo hanashitai.*" (Excuse me. I want to speak Japanese.)

When I raised my head, the expression of bewilderment had not left his face. But he started speaking Japanese to me, explaining that he hadn't spoken the language since 1945 and had vowed to himself that he never would again, but that because I was an American and not a Japanese it was all right. (For years before and during the war, Koreans were forced to speak Japanese, the language of their colonizers.)

So every day, when I returned to the inn in the late afternoon after my wanderings about the city of Seoul, the old proprietor and I would have an hour-long conversation in Japanese. (Years later, my dear friend, playwright and novelist Inoue Hisashi said to me, "You had the best possible teacher of Japanese—a Korean.")

In late October my visa came through, and it was a great relief. I had precious little money left and had been filled with anxiety that I would be turned down and have to spend the rest of my life

THE PUZZLE COMES TOGETHER

wandering from one Asian country to another.

I will never forget the day I again met President Araki to sign my teaching contract. He had asked me to meet him in a restaurant in the Imperial Hotel in Tokyo. This was, of course, the old Imperial Hotel designed by Frank Lloyd Wright, the one that had withstood the earthquake that ravaged Tokyo just before noon on September 1, 1923, the very day the hotel was officially opened. Sadly this fabulous architectural monument, which today would no doubt be a World Heritage Site, was torn down the next year, with the entrance and lobby moved to the historical theme park at Meiji Mura where they were reassembled.

As I walked through the entrance of the Imperial Hotel on that crisp late autumn day, I felt as if I had snatched personal happiness from the jaws of despair. I had hopped over a huge pothole on the road that was my life and landed on my feet on the other side. I can still see in my mind's eye the old molded beige stones of the hotel walls and that wonderful temple-like entrance inviting me in for what was one of the rites of passage into my new life.

"Hello, President Araki," I said to him, mistakenly using the word for "president" that describes the head of state of the United States of America.

"Oh," he said. "I can see that you've learned some Japanese, even if you do speak with a Korean accent."

This set in motion the series of events of a kind that a person is often not able to control. You pack your bag, buy a ticket to a new city, find a place to live and start a new job. Everything seems decided for you by someone else. This life came upon you. You did not choose it. You certainly didn't plan it. As for me, I was more than happy to let this happen, to let events carry me along and wash over me. For that past year in Eastern and Western Europe and the U.S., I felt as if I had been tossed about by an invisible wave, lifted high in the air on its crest and then dumped, with a thud, back to earth.

But the important thing is that you must let it happen to you. You may be utterly restless. Your life may appear to be directionless.

But you put yourself in a position where chance might just pass before you; and, what is crucial, you recognize that chance when it appears in a flash in front of you and you grab hold of it. If you are too timid or too afraid to take the risk of reaching out to it and grasping it, or if you hesitate for too long, that chance will pass you by and appear before someone else.

The greatest thing that ever happened in my life was my coming to Japan and being able to live and work here. That was possible because I could speak and teach two foreign languages. So, my study of Russian and Polish took on a meaning that I could never have anticipated. In the end, that's why I studied those languages—to be able to live in Japan.

That's how the jigsaw puzzle of life gets put together. The individual pieces, always out of order, will make no sense solely by themselves.

3

RESPONSIBILITY FOR THE PAST

Why did I consider Japan my country at such an early stage? Was this a case of unrequited love? If you asked the Japanese who knew me, they would all say in unison, "Roger is not a Japanese." Even if I became a Japanese citizen and changed my name (which was required by law), Japanese people would still refuse to consider me a "real" Japanese. I could not, in the eyes of the Japanese people, become a Japanese. Yet, I still felt deep in my bones—where it counts—that this was my country. But why?

Why do we fall in love with someone? We think we know the reasons, but most of them are rationalizations of a raw and instinctive emotion, one that originates not in the brain but in the heart, among other organs.

At first I wasn't smitten by all of Japan, just with one very small and reputedly mysterious corner of it. Located at that corner in the northern district of Kyoto was an ancient pond whose name is pronounced in a number of ways: Midorogaike, Midoroike, Mizorogaike and Mizoroike. As its *kanji*, or written characters, suggest, it is a "Deep Muddy Pond."

I say mysterious because this pond, which indeed does have a very deep quicksand-like mud bed, is actually a swamp, with rare flora such as insectivorous plants and *junsai*, or watershield, a delicacy you find in the *suimono*, or clear soups, and miso soups accompanying a Japanese meal. In fact, the junsai of the Deep Muddy Pond was once valued as being of the highest quality in Japan; and it is a shame that, due to pollution of the pond's water, they ceased harvesting these slippery young plants of the native water lily, enveloped in an agar-like jelly, even years before I arrived there.

At night an eerie dark settled over the bushes and trees around the pond, and people in the area believed that a ghost made appearances there. More than a few taxi drivers told me that they had delivered a beautiful young woman to the shore of the pond, only to find that she had disappeared from the back seat before the car door was opened, leaving a little puddle where she had been.

I came to live in a tiny yellow house at Midoroikecho, just a stone's throw from the pond. Three or four minutes' walk up the narrow road that ran by my house was a famous temple, Entsuji, which boasts an exquisite moss and rock garden. This garden is renown in Japan for incorporating Mt. Hiei into it, thanks to the principle of *shakkei*, or borrowed scenery. The very idea that something outside a garden could be seen as a part of it excited me, and I visited Entsuji about once a week and got to know the old monk there, who had a reputation for being exceedingly cantankerous.

Three years after moving to Midoroikecho, the monk officiated at my wedding ceremony overlooking that stunning garden, a "wedding on borrowed scenery."

My wife was a young Norwegian named Solrun. She had come from Oslo University to Kyoto University for post-graduate studies. Solrun eventually became a first-rate filmmaker of both ethnographic films, primarily in Okinawa, and one feature film, titled *Aya*. Solrun and I didn't have any children, separated in 1980 and divorced in 1983. I was crushed when she died suddenly of a heart attack in Melbourne in December 2009.

Before meeting Solrun in the autumn of 1969, I had been on a solitary journey of discovery of the culture of my new country, and I traveled to every nook and cranny of Kyoto on my 200cc red and black Yamaha motorcycle. These discoveries formed the basis of my first book of short stories, *On the Edge of Kyoto*, published by Asahi Press.

I rode my motorcycle up to Tsuruga on the coast of the Sea of Japan, to see if there was anything left of the Russian presence there. Tsuruga had been a major port for Russian ships. In fact, I saw many faded Russian signs on book shops, clothing stores and restaurants, and was intrigued by the old Russian consulate, which, as I hoisted myself up the fence, I could peer straight into.

The most exciting trips were by train to Kyushu (few people flew domestically in Japan in those days), where I went from town to village in search of Kyushu's links with the cultures of the Asian continent. On one trip, in 1968, I started at Usuki, then hitchhiked down to Miyazaki, Kirishima National Park, Kagoshima and, a city I fell in love with, Nagasaki.

I often met with my mentor, Professor Wakaizumi, at the university's Kamigamo campus, which was not far from my home by the pond. Professor Wakaizumi had invited the world-famous historian Arnold Toynbee to give a talk at Sandai, and he asked if I would act as a guide and interpreter for him and his wife, Veronica. Toynbee was particularly popular among Asian scholars because he had professed the decline of the West. (I also acted as interpreter for Profs. Toynbee and Wakaizumi when they collaborated on their book, *Surviving the Future*, published by Oxford University Press in 1971.)

I went with the Toynbees to Nara, where we stayed at the beautiful old Nara Hotel, built in 1909. Professor Toynbee, nearly eighty, a quiet and reserved man, was entirely at home in Japan, but his wife, Veronica, was not at all satisfied with things she saw here, criticizing Japanese people for being "too Western." (This was a common mistake made by many Europeans, who, ever since the days of Lafcadio Hearn, had preferred Japanese to be quaintly traditional, ceremonious and decorative.)

The straw that broke the camel's back for her was breakfast.

We were taking our breakfast in the elegant hotel dining room. The waiters came to our table toting enormous silver trays adorned with Western-style breakfasts of bacon, eggs, toast, fruit and cornflakes. Mrs. Toynbee would have none of it.

"What's this?! Why are we being served an American breakfast? Roger, ask the waiters."

I asked the waiters if this was the usual breakfast at the Nara Hotel. They naturally replied that it was.

This made Mrs. Toynbee, an Englishwoman born in the Victorian era and not at all well disposed to "Orientals acting like Americans," even more incensed.

"Roger. You tell them to take these cornflakes and whatever. Tell them I want sushi and sashimi and tempura. Really!"

As guide and interpreter I had no choice but to translate her words; and the waiters took away all three breakfasts. (I would have been very happy to eat such a wonderful American breakfast.) I don't know how they did it, but after a while the waiters brought us sushi, sashimi and tempura. I didn't eat the sashimi. It looked considerably over the hill. The chefs at the Nara Hotel in 1968 were very clever to be able to come up with these "Japanese" dishes so early in the morning.

Professor Toynbee was delighted with Japan's recent successes. That year Japan's economy surpassed that of West Germany, to become the second largest among democratic countries. He had a perspective that went far back to before the First World War, and had been a delegate at the Paris Peace Conference in 1919. He had also been in Smyrna when the city was set alight and destroyed by the Turkish army in 1922. (Many people have forgotten that a Japanese ship, the Tokei Maru, jettisoned its entire valuable cargo to rescue survivors in the water, while Allied ships were still refusing to take them on. The ship took on as many refugees as possible, some eight hundred and twenty, and transported them to safety in Piraeus.)

Professor Toynbee, born just six days before Hitler on April 14, 1889, had witnessed, as both journalist and historian, two world wars and the decline of empires. He denounced the notion that nuclear weapons were a deterrent to war, seeing them as comprising an existential threat that might lead to "the self-liquidation of our species." In this view he found much common ground with the only people in the world who have suffered the effects of atomic bombs.

Professor Wakaizumi's most striking guest at Sandai, however, was the world-famous American futurologist, Herman Kahn.

Again I was asked to be interpreter and guide for Professor Kahn and his wife, Jane. (Kahn introduced his wife to me as "a very right-wing American.")

Herman Kahn was a military strategist who came to Japan praising the country as the new superpower. He was the great geo-strategist, the ultimate doomsday game-theory player and one of the models for Peter Sellers's character of Dr. Strangelove in Stanley Kubrick's 1964 movie of that name, subtitled *How I Learned to Stop Worrying and Love the Bomb.*

Unlike Professor Toynbee, Kahn believed that nuclear war was not only highly likely, but winnable. He wrote and spoke of "tolerable" levels of victims in the tens of millions. It may not be widely known now that Herman Kahn became a self-styled expert on Japan, co-authoring *The Japanese Challenge* in 1979. But when he came to Japan in 1969—the year I interpreted for him—he knew precious little about this country.

His visit was welcomed by those in the highest echelons of the Liberal Democratic Party. Prime Minister Sato Eisaku was facing a difficult election the coming January, and Kahn's rosy predictions about the rise of a Japanese superstate gave comfort to his party. Kahn praised Japan and its leadership to the hilt. Japanese people's opinions are vulnerable to influence from the outside. A prominent American could have more sway in the country than a Japanese politician. (This is still the case, to a large extent.)

But when we went to Osaka for him to give a talk to entrepreneurs in that commercial center, his theories about Japan leading the world into the twenty-first century were greeted with skeptical grimaces. The Osaka business world has traditionally been much less ideological than its Tokyo counterpart; and "the American expert's" opinions on Japan were taken with a very large grain of salt.

One evening during their visit, Herman Kahn, his wife Jane and I had dinner in Kyoto at my favorite tempura restaurant just off Kiyamachi, the narrow street alongside the Takase River. The Takase River is celebrated in Mori Ogai's classic short story of that name, "Takasegawa."

"This country will go nuclear by 1985," he said to me. "You can't have an economic superstate without the nuclear deterrent. And despite what the businessmen in Osaka said, Japan will overtake the U.S. as an economic power by the turn of the century."

"Well, that's a long way off," I said, trying to imagine what life in Japan would be like by the turn of the century more than thirty years hence. "But the nuclear allergy here is pretty strong."

"It won't last two decades." Having said that, he looked around the restaurant, then glared at me over the top rim of his glasses.

"But Roger, let me ask you a question."

"Sure."

"What are you doing here working for the Japanese?"

"I'm lecturing at Kyoto Sangyo University in Russian and Polish. What do you mean? I live here. I love it here. I don't consider myself to be 'working for the Japanese.' Take this food, tempura. It's Japanese food, but what's the difference? If you like it, you like it. It can be yours as well as anybody else's."

I wasn't being very articulate in my defense of my Japanese life, and he came back with something quite incisive.

"It's an acquired taste. Just like your feelings about Japan. You are an American and it's that simple. You may like it here, but you don't belong here."

Now it was not only the Japanese people who were telling me this was not my country, it was an American, and a very famous one at that.

Herman Kahn spoke much about America during the few days in 1969 that I spent with him and his wife. He was a prototype of the present-day neocon, an unstinting advocate of absolute American values. His game-theorizing about a nuclear holocaust was bold and global; but when it came down to it, he was an American patriot posing as an internationalist. I realized that a lot of American people of influence praise Japan only in order for the Japanese to support the U.S. more vociferously. Their praise of Japan has ulterior motives, motives that the Japanese generally see through but are too timid, or intimidated, to challenge.

The most frightening thing of all—and the reason why I write about Herman Kahn here—is that he thought he could understand a country, in this case Japan, without learning a thing about its culture or lifestyle, its spirit and heart. His worldview was a blend of strategy, subterfuge and ruse. During the several days we spent together, virtually from morning till night, he didn't ask me one single question about the culture of Japan. How different this was from Arnold Toynbee, with whom I had spent much less time. Professor Toynbee was fascinated by Kyoto and wanted to know how I felt about the contribution that Japanese culture was making to Japan's social and economic successes. Of course, he felt that the East was eventually going to rise again to rival the West. The transformations that Japan were going through gave credence to this belief. Japan at the time was like China today: ostensibly unstoppable.

I have always been wary of experts who assert the partiality for a foreign culture as an "acquired taste." Futurologist Herman Kahn died in 1983, never to see that his prediction about Japan becoming a nuclear power two years later did not come true. Nor had Japan overtaken the United States by the turn of the new century.

My memories of Wakaizumi Kei are much deeper and more complex than those associated with our two illustrious guests. And a few years ago they came rushing back to me with great force.

On March 9, 2010, a panel of experts appointed by Foreign Minister Okada Katsuya presented its findings on secret agreements made between Japan and the United States with regard to the revision of the Japan-U.S. Security Treaty in 1960 and the reversion of Okinawa to Japan in 1972. This revealed some salient details of those pacts that contravened the three non-nuclear principles: never to possess, manufacture or permit the introduction into Japanese territory of nuclear weapons.

Those principles, adopted as a parliamentary resolution in 1971, but never enshrined in law, forbid Japan from possessing or producing nuclear weapons or permitting them to be on its territory. The two main secret pacts in contravention of those principles are a 1960 agreement allowing nuclear-armed U.S. planes and ships to enter Japan, and one from 1969 regarding the reversion of Okinawa to Japan and the possible presence of such weapons there.

Despite these blatant transgressions of Japan's non-nuclear principles, Japanese leaders have consistently denied the existence of the agreements, in effect pulling the wool over the public's eyes. The plot only thickened as former LDP prime ministers rushed to defend prevarication in the name of "patriotism."

Wakaizumi Kei, my mentor during those early years in Japan, figures significantly in this issue. When I met him at the Kyoto Sangyo University Sendagaya office in Tokyo in 1967, he was in his late thirties, suave, polite and soft spoken.

Born in Fukui prefecture in 1930, Professor Wakaizumi was a political science graduate from the University of Tokyo who had spent a formative year in 1960 as a visiting scholar at Johns Hopkins University in Baltimore, Maryland.

Professor Wakaizumi's link with the secret pact came about at the urging of Henry Kissinger, President Richard Nixon's national security adviser. Then a special envoy to Prime Minister Sato, Professor Wakaizumi accompanied the prime minister to Washington; and, on November 21, 1969, the two of them went to the White House, where they were called by Nixon into a private room. There, the prime minister and the president signed a secret document, witnessed by Professor Wakaizumi, that granted the U.S. the right, with consultation, to bring nuclear weapons in an emergency into Okinawa after its reversion to Japan. (Only four people knew of the existence of this pact that violated Japan's non-nuclear principles, the fourth being Kissinger.)

On September 21, 1971, when asked about the status of American nuclear weapons in post-reversion Okinawa, White House Press Secretary Ronald Ziegler said, "It is our policy not to reveal the presence of nuclear weapons overseas."

Over time I noticed a change taking place in Professor

Wakaizumi's demeanor. He seemed to be under enormous stress. He took a long break to return to Fukui where, he told me, he sat Zen at Eiheiji, the Zen temple in his native Fukui prefecture founded in the thirteenth century by the revered scholar and monk Dogen. At the time, of course, I had no idea of the strain he was under by virtue of his role in the secret pact.

I left Kyoto to take up a teaching position in Australia in 1972 and, for a time, lost contact with him. It was some years before I came to know about the pressure the LDP had put on him as he struggled to come to terms with an ever-growing guilt.

In 1994, the leading conservative publishing house Bungeishunju published his memoir under a title that translates as "I Had No Recourse." In the course of six hundred pages he pours out his heart not only about the secret pact but also regarding his vision for the future of Japan.

Of course, he knew all too well that the LDP-led government would not take kindly to his confessions concerning his role in the Nixon-Sato agreement. The last time I saw him was in the late 1980s, when I believe he was either contemplating or already writing his memoir. He had had what amounted to a nervous breakdown. I still did not, at that stage, know why, but could tell that his nerves were in a delicate state.

I believe that the secret agreement was signed because LDP leaders have wanted—and still want—to destroy Japan's antinuclear allergy and acquire a nuclear capability for the country, making Herman Kahn's ominous prediction a reality.

After his book came out, Professor Wakaizumi traveled to Okinawa with a note in his pocket addressed to the Okinawan people. In the note he revealed his sense of "grave responsibility" for his part in the deception. He also carried a knife with which he intended to kill himself at a cemetery for the war dead. He did not attempt suicide, but instead, deeply depressed and regretful of his role in the blatant duplicity of his leaders, went down to Ishigaki Isle in the Yaeyama Islands, the southernmost part of Okinawa prefecture, where he rested and strove to regain composure. Two years later, wracked with guilt, he drank poison, taking his own life at his family home in Fukui.

Wakaizumi Kei was a conservative in politics, and I knew that we did not see eye to eye on many issues, particularly the war in Vietnam. For this reason, I never brought up such subjects. But he was a man with a real conscience who came to see that he had to take personal responsibility for his actions. I admire him immensely. He represents the best qualities of the Japanese people: the ability to come to terms with your mistakes and acknowledge them, then try to make amends as best as you can, whatever the personal cost.

Sadly, he took his life in an act of repentance, and Japan lost an honest man of deep conscience. I lost a dear, kind and wonderful mentor and friend.

The world needs this Japan now more than ever, the Japan that is honest, forthright and full of compassion, with Japanese people willing to change their opinions and make amends according to their principles. If this is not done, Japan will never become reconciled with their neighbors in East Asia.

I knew by becoming a Japanese in my heart, I had to accept this country's past as well as its present. I had to feel a sense of responsibility for what occurred here over the twentieth century, just as if I was a young Japanese person. Not having been alive when Japan sent troops to invade countries in Asia and the Pacific would not let me off the hook. I would have to come to terms with the Japanese mindset of the past, as well as that of the present, in a personal way.

It was this sense of responsibility, felt deep in my bones, that made me, more than anything, if only in my own eyes, a Japanese.

4
COMPLETE IMPERFECTION

The longer I lived in Kyoto, the more I came to feel on my home ground in Japan. But to me, the soul of Kyoto did not reside in the famous temples of the city. Nor did I sense any feeling of belonging in Gosho, the old imperial palace, or Heian Shrine, or even in Entsuji's garden, with its exquisite low mounds of moss, waves on a sea of white stones. It was that wild and mysterious place called Midorogaike, the Deep Muddy Pond, that captured me.

Midorogaike was my Japanese garden. I walked around it two or three times a week. Back in the late '60s you could see a little wooden boat sunken into the mud that formed the bed of the pond. The mud is actually several yards deep. The boat had belonged to Maruya, the shop that harvested the watershield for Kyoto's finicky restaurateurs.

Seeing that little boat half-submerged in mud prompted me to think about what comprised the beauty of Japan. On the one hand, here you had Midorogaike, an entirely natural landscape, a swamp, similar to the one at Ota Shrine not far away in Kamigamo, where the irises have been famous since the time they were celebrated in the *Shinkokinshu*, the collection of poems compiled at the beginning of the thirteenth century. Apparently Arigaike, a small pond also in Kamigamo and now part of a golf course, is part of the complex of these two swamps.

Wild, natural Midorogaike ... and a few minutes' walk away, the *karesansui*, or "waterless," garden at Entsuji, exquisitely and meticulously fashioned by an artist. These are the two extremes of the Japanese aesthetic, the one left *sonomama*, or "as is," and the other totally created by the hand of a human using the components of nature.

And yet, they are the same in one way.

I began in those early Kyoto days to think about the meaning of the simple phrase sonomama. It may be the closest Japanese word to "natural." *Shizenteki* or *shizenno*, the words generally considered equivalent to "natural," don't come as close as sonomama. Sonomama even looks natural on the page, made up not of kanji like the word *shizen* but of four simple *hiragana*. Hiragana, the native Japanese alphabet, has a softer look to it than kanji, which were imported from China and are often more conceptual and solid in effect.

Midorogaike's beauty is certainly derived from nature "as is." The beauty of nearby Entsuji's garden may not be sonomama, but the creator's aspiration was to fashion something that *looked* like nature.

At first glance, Japanese art tends to twist things, to warp things, to *ijiru* (fiddle with) what is natural. But the goal is to twist and warp and ijiru to such an extent that you take the object from its sonomama state through a series of transformations until you come full circle back again to something resembling sonomama. You create the new sonomama, turning "as is" into "as was." By doing this, you make the passage of time an integral element of the work itself.

There is a common phrase in Japanese that describes complete perfection: *kanzen-muketsu*. This is one goal of Western art, to create a beauty that is complete, perfect and enduring. What comes to mind is John Keats's poem beginning "A thing of beauty is a joy forever."

But the goal of Japanese art is different. It is to create something that does not last, that fades with time and expresses the fleeting nature of life. Its message is *shogyo-mujo*, the Buddhist precept that "all is vanity and evanescence." There is no such thing as permanence. A thing of beauty is a joy for *now*, allowing you to appreciate, savor and live more fully in this moment in time. Japanese art seeks to reveal truth and beauty to the observer in an instant, before the doors close again and it is no longer seen—until the next artistic revelation shines a light before your eyes.

COMPLETE IMPERFECTION

Japanese art does not aim to be perfect, because nature itself—and here by nature I mean sonomama—is never perfect. So, the essence of Japanese art is not kanzen-muketsu, but an expression that I coined to illustrate the principle: *kanzen-yuketsu*, or complete *im*perfection.

Many wonderful examples of art or artistic practice that symbolize kanzen-yuketsu come to mind. In the tea ceremony, in some senses the epitome of Japanese aesthetic realization, the order of value in tea bowls is generally said to be "first Raku, second Hagi, third Karatsu." These three names designate kilns in three different districts of Japan. Nothing could be more symbolic of kanzen-yuketsu than a *raku-chawan*, or Raku-ware tea bowl. The name comes from a palace, Jurakudai, built in the sixteenth century by Japan's most powerful leader at that time, Toyotomi Hideyoshi. These Raku-ware bowls are not made on a wheel, which would urge symmetry into clay; but rather they are fashioned with the hands and a pallet. It always amazes foreigners how very expensive these "imperfect" little bowls can be.

Hagi and Karatsu tea bowls are also *soboku*. (Soboku, a highly nuanced word meaning "artless and unadorned," relates deeply to Japanese aesthetics.) With this type of Japanese ceramics, the "accidents" that occur in the hand or the wheel or the kiln become all important. These accidents create the art. Seconds may harbor more artistic value than firsts. In Western ceramic art the goal is to achieve perfection. Ceramics that come out of the kiln as seconds are either sold cheaply or tossed on a pile.

The tea ceremony itself displays a "fetish of rusticity." In what other country would you actually choose to sit uncomfortably in a small space gazing at such simple and imperfect things as the various textures of wood in the room, from the ceiling to the pillar in the tokonoma (alcove) to the plain tea whisk itself. Tea in the West is an elegant affair with tasteful or ornate cups and saucers served in an opulent setting. Kanzen-yuketsu is the very negation of opulence.

The art of calligraphy as it has been practiced in Japan over the centuries is imperfection raised to an art. Some characters or *kana* script are so imperfect you can't read them! They look like squiggles on the surface of an action painting.

Finally, the sounds created in much traditional Japanese music, particularly that of the shakuhachi, incorporate kanzen-yuketsu. How do they do this? It is the trailing off of the sound into silence that is just as important, if not more important, than the sound itself. It is at the point in between, when neither sound nor silence are heard, that the heart is moved.

All of this ties in with my notion of "the design of time" (See Chapter 16). Kanzen-yuketsu plays a vital role in this because it brings to the eye, the ear, the nose, the tongue and the skin a realization of the passage of time and our sensual appreciation of it.

If kanzen-yuketsu seems to be a paradox, well, it is. Japanese art at its best is paradoxical. It contains the arcane within the artless, darkness within light, the moment within an eternity, death within a life.

This is what occurred to me as I walked, sometimes at twilight—perhaps hoping to meet up with that elusive ghost—around the deep and muddy pond, my symbol of the Japan in me. Yet, needless to say, there had to be more in Japan than a single pond. I spent as much free time as I had traveling in the countryside, always with the goal in mind of transplanting Japanese culture into my marrow. At Usuki in Oita prefecture I saw the rock Buddhas from the Kamakura period (1185-1333) carved into the mountainsides, and stayed on Kuroshima in Usuki Bay, the little island where Englishman William Adams, known in Japan as Miura Anjin, first set foot on Japanese soil in the year 1600. I journeyed twice to Onta and Koishiwara, also in Oita prefecture, to visit the *noborigama* (climbing kilns), where earth is pounded by *karausu*, huge pestles that strike mortars dug into the ground. This is where British potter Bernard Leach was inspired by ceramics that have been made there for more than three centuries. As you walk through the village, you hear the sound of the karausu coming down with a shriek and a thud, like beasts crying out as they trample the earth.

Each time at Onta and Koishiwara I bought plates and bowls and sake jugs. I went to the little town of Nakatsu to visit the home in which the great author of the Japanese enlightenment, Fukuzawa Yukichi, lived. But it was not only such intellectual and aesthetic activities that drew me to Kyushu. I will never forget the most fantastic sushi at Tenzushi, the renowned sushi restaurant at Kokura in northern Kyushu, where they didn't serve sake because "it spoils the pure flavor of the sushi."

In southern Shikoku I went to the birthplace of John Manjiro in the village of Nakahama. He is also known as Nakahama Manjiro. In 1841, when Manjiro was fourteen, the fishing boat that he and four friends were on capsized, and they were picked up by an American whaler and taken to the United States. This was during Japan's period of national isolation, when even attempting to leave the country was punishable by death. Manjiro did return to Japan after spending a decade in the U.S., however, eventually becoming a famous author and translator who contributed in a major way to Japan's modernization.

I came to love Japanese onsen, or hot springs; and, in the autumn of 1968, took a bus from the Kii Peninsula coast to the remote village of Ryujin (Dragon God), famous for its waters, later hitchhiking from there over the mountains of Wakayama prefecture to sacred Mt. Koya. I took a particular interest in folk performance and traveled to many country festivals, especially those where some kind of traditional play or dance was performed. I recall a particularly spectacular festival, the Shimotsuki Matsuri, where enormous bonfires are lit at night along the Tenryu River south of that beautiful old town of many inns, Iida, in Nagano prefecture, and an endless stream of sparks shot into the black sky. I went to Neo Village in Gifu prefecture for performances of Nogo *sarugaku*, an old form of noh drama originating in China.

In order to understand the noh, I felt I had to first understand its roots. In Japan you can observe several forms of a theatrical genre going back centuries. The Japanese culture is an agglutinative one. New forms don't entirely replace old ones. They are tacked onto them. Nearby was the famous cherry blossom tree called Usuzumizakura, which is allegedly more than 1,500 years old, defying both nature and my allegation that in Japan a thing of beauty is not a joy forever. "Usuzumi" is a kind of play on words that can mean "Faint Life"; so the name itself recognizes that this gorgeous old tree is only living on thanks to the capricious blessing of nature.

I went to Nagahama in Shiga prefecture on the shores of Lake Biwa to see the theater performed by little boys, Hikiyama Kyogen. Though it is called kyogen, a form of comic relief performed together with noh plays, it is really a type of kabuki. I journeyed to Aichi prefecture with actor Ozawa Shoichi to see Mikawa Manzai, another traditional folk dramatic art, performed on tatami mats in an old farmhouse.

I traveled twice up to Kurokawa in Yamagata prefecture, once to see the all-night noh performances in February, where you walk from one farmhouse to another in the middle of the night and the snow is piled up to your shoulders along the sides of the road. This was fifty years ago now. The farmhouse theaters were packed with people, and once you secured your tiny space on the tatami to squeeze into, you had to stay there. If you went out for a pee, your place would be gone in a few wiggles of the people sitting around you. I returned in the summer of 1971 to see the *mushiboshi* of the masks and costumes. (Mushiboshi is a fascinating term for "airing out." Literally it means "the drying out of the insects.")

I took a boat trip from Miyako on the Rikuchu Coast in Iwate prefecture, that town so tragically devastated by the earthquake and tsunami in March 2011, up to Kuji, to visit the potters there. Alas, my only *kokuji*-ware bowl, a beautiful creamy white one, smashed to the floor of my home in Sydney in 2006. I made it a point to return years later to replace it with an even more beautiful one, which now has pride of place at home. The wildflowers dotting the cliffs of the Rikuchu Coast stand out vividly in my mind. And the wakame seaweed, squid and sea squirt (a Tohoku delicacy) from there are still the best I have ever had. (I am a big fan of sea squirt and always rib my Tokyo friends when they profess that they can't eat this Japanese food that smells somewhat like the pungent durian. It is usually us foreigners who are chided for not being able to swallow one Japanese dish or another.)

Then there was the trip to the Shimokita Peninsula at the northernmost tip of the main island of Honshu. I took a little boat from Aomori to Hotokegaura, those strangely Buddha-shaped rocks rising up from the shore, picking sea urchin right out of the water there, slicing them open and eating them with a spoon. The photo of me at age twenty-six that appears on the back cover of the Australian edition of my play *Yamashita* was taken at Hotokegaura.

From the western edge of the Shimokita Peninsula at Hotokegaura, I hopped on a bus and eventually reached the top of the holy mountain Osorezan at the time when the *miko*, or shamanesses, were acting as media for messages, conveyed in gruff low voices, from the departed to loved ones who wished to communicate with them. The sulphurous smoke emanating from the shallow lake at the summit of the cratered mountain carried its own messages from the other world.

Of course, many people have traveled more extensively than this. I record these recollections here only to show you that Japan has retained its various pasts. They coexist with the present. Few countries in the world—perhaps no country in the world—can boast such startling cultural *contemporary* riches as Japan as seen in performance-based festivals that have been a continual feature of the landscape for, in some cases, close to a millennium. That few Japanese people appreciate these, and that some of this wonderful artistic and theatrical legacy is being lost around Japan today, is a tragedy of immense proportions, not only for Japan but for the world.

Oh yes—if these festivals were officially recognized by the world, then Japanese people would stand up and take notice, and maybe be proud of their country's traditions. Why do these things depend so much on outside recognition?

Too often Japanese people rely on such recognition for their self-esteem. This is a ridiculous form of inverted pride. It is time for Japanese people to delve into their own traditions, support them, participate in them and be utterly proud of them, whatever people in America, Europe, China or anywhere else think about them. People in the Meiji era did have that kind of pride. But tragically, the aggressive chauvinism of the colonial period, roughly from 1895 to 1945, claimed cultural "superiority" as a weapon in its arsenal; and pride in tradition was lost in the pernicious association. It is a sign of Japan's silent remorse for the crimes the nation committed in Asia and the Pacific that such pride is shunned. But it is high time to separate the legacy of militaristic colonialism from the culture.

Perhaps my greatest trips, and ones I could call pilgrimages, were to Hanamaki, the small town in Iwate prefecture where poet and author Miyazawa Kenji was born. Hanamaki is where I found the inspiration to write this book.

After living in Japan for a few months, I started to feel confident in my spoken Japanese. I spent every waking hour, when I wasn't teaching, learning Japanese, and avoiding encounters with other foreigners so that I could speak as much as possible with Japanese people, any Japanese people, even some startlingly boring ones. Mastering Japanese was my primary goal, at any cost.

But I realized, naturally, that I would never know the language—any language—if I couldn't read it. So I asked a close friend, Abe Tetsuzo, professor of French at Kyoto Institute of Technology, "Who writes the most beautiful Japanese?" He answered, "Well, it's got to be Miyazawa Kenji."

I rushed down to Maruzen bookstore on Kawaramachi Boulevard in downtown Kyoto (sadly, this bookstore is no longer there) and bought a collection of Kenji's stories. When I opened it, I was in for a shock. Though I could read ordinary Japanese prose by then, I couldn't follow the logic of the style. I picked what looked like the shortest story, a mere three pages, "The Story of the Zashiki Bokko," and started reading it, determined to get as far as I could without a dictionary. I gave in halfway through the first page and used my dictionary, but, even so, the first page still took nearly two hours to get through. I managed to finish this story, which gave me a great sense of achievement. Just finishing it was enough. I didn't really understand it at that time.

Many years later I translated this eerily lyrical story about a boy no one could see, modeled on the *zashiki warashi*, the elusive "tatami imp" of Iwate. I was fascinated by Kenji's use of mimetic words and phrases in Japanese, and from about 1968, I started to call him Miyazawa-zawa Kenji, because *zawa-zawa* means "rustling," as in "rustling leaves." It is the sound a broom makes on the tatami, or the footsteps of an invisible boy....

As my reading ability grew, I read more and more works of prose and poetry by Miyazawa-zawa Kenji, and the more I read, the more I fell in love with his use of language and the deep spirit of compassion permeating his work. It started me on a journey of study that has lasted half a century; and I am still plumbing the depths in the poems and stories of this writer who I consider one of the greatest of the twentieth century in any country of the world.

At that time, and right up to the 1990s, Kenji was not considered a "representative" of Japanese literature. His works were generally not studied at the major American universities where Japanese literature is taught. The famous professors of those universities classified Kenji as a children's author of "fantasy literature" who was not as important as those towering figures of early modern Japanese literature, such as Natsume Soseki and Mori Ogai.

This was a time—the late 1960s—when Mishima Yukio was still alive and writing; and the pre-eminent figure of postwar literature, Tanizaki Jun'ichiro, had died only a few years previous to that. I remember well when Mishima brought out the fourth volume of his tetralogy, *The Sea of Fertility*. I also recall with perfect clarity watching him live on television delivering his speech to the stunned members of the Self-Defense Forces on the balcony at Ichigaya in Tokyo. I was having lunch in the Sandai staff cafeteria at the time. After the short speech, he entered the building through a window adjacent to the balcony and slit open his belly. One of the retainers in his self-styled private militia, the Shield Society, delivered the coup de grace by slicing off his head with a sword.

Kawabata Yasunari received the Nobel Prize in Literature in 1968. And whether you asked those famous professors at their American universities or virtually any member of the Japanese literary establishment who the three greatest living or recently deceased Japanese authors were, you would invariably get the answer, Tanizaki Jun'ichiro, Kawabata Yasunari and Mishima Yukio. Alas, by the time I left Japan for Australia in August 1972, all three were dead, Kawabata, like Mishima, by his own hand.

When people asked me who I thought was the greatest Japanese writer, I always answered "Miyazawa Kenji"; and they looked at me with a face that is well described in the Japanese phrase "as if their deep-fried tofu was snatched from them by a buzzard"—that is, totally flabbergasted. Some of them said to me, "Do you mean Mizoguchi Kenji?" Mizoguchi was, of course, the renown film director.

I decided, as I always did, that I had to see Kenji's birthplace in order to understand his writings. So I set out from Kyoto to Tokyo by shinkansen, and then by ordinary express train to Hanamaki. This was in the summer of 1969, long before the arrival of the Tohoku shinkansen.

Just outside the entrance of Hanamaki Station there was a little information booth. I asked the young lady in the booth where Miyazawa Kenji's house was, and she was kind enough to draw me a map. I walked to the house, and when I arrived there, I was in for a big shock. The nameplate on the pillar beside the front gate read "Miyazawa." Oh my God, I thought, was Miyazawa Kenji still alive? I was sure he had died in 1933 but....

I stood under the eaves of the house, slid open the front door a few inches and said, "*Gomen kudasai!* (Excuse me!)."

A man in his mid-sixties immediately came to the door. He looked surprised to see a foreigner.

"Excuse me. I am from America and I love Miyazawa Kenji!"

It was an illustration of just that variety of innocence and chutzpah that characterized my personality at the time.

The man who answered the door turned out to be Kenji's younger brother, Miyazawa Seiroku. As is well known, he had been very close to his brother and at age twenty-nine, being some eight years younger than Kenji, had been with him at his deathbed in 1933. Seiroku was exceedingly kind to me, talking a lot about Kenji and taking me by car to various places in and around Hanamaki. When we stood on the English Coast overlooking the Kitakami River, I felt for a moment that I was with Miyazawa Kenji himself.

I saw Seiroku a number of times over the years in both Hanamaki and Tokyo. The last time was in August 2000. This was a year before he died at age ninety-seven. He had lived a life sixty years longer than that of his brother. I had come up to Hanamaki in 2000 to take my son, Jeremy, on a trip to Tohoku. Seiroku, though very weak and confined to bed, generously let us into his bedroom. When we walked in, he sat up in bed with great difficultly, and, in that voice which people used to say was very much like Kenji's, quoted the first line of one of his brother's poems about the sparkles of light on the Kitakami River. I came back with the second line. (We had always quoted the first two lines of this poem to each other when we met.) I introduced Jeremy to him, and he slowly stretched out his frail hand.

Despite the impression I have been giving, I didn't spend all my time traveling, eating sea urchin and watching ancient rituals in remote country villages. I decided to read every major work of modern Japanese literature. As my reading ability improved, I devoured Soseki, Ogai, Izumi Kyoka and Akutagawa Ryunosuke; Dazai Osamu, Oda Sakunosuke and Sakaguchi Ango; Ibuse Masuji, Ooka Shohei, Takeda Taijun ... and the works of many other writers. Little did I know that in a matter of only two or three years' time I would be teaching Japanese literature in, of all places, Australia, taking the biggest leap I was ever to take.

Whatever I read, I always turned back to my first passion, the works of Miyazawa Kenji. Actress Nagaoka Teruko, who was born not far from Hanamaki in Morioka in 1908 (and lived to the grand old age of 102), was reading Kenji's longest work of prose, *Night on the Milky Way Train* on NHK radio, and listening to her went a long way to help me understand that masterpiece. (I was fortunate to be able to meet her in 2006 and tell her how much her reading at that time had meant to me.)

I started to translate this novel—the best way to understand a story is to translate it—finishing my first version in 1971. As I looked back some years later, it was all too apparent that it was pretty horrible and full of textual errors. I retranslated the novel in 1982 and published it as a weekly serial in the *Mainichi Daily News*, where I was working as literary editor. This became the second serialization of a Japanese novel in a Japanese English-language daily. The first had been the translation I did of Inoue Hisashi's satirical novel about the trials of a foreign man of the cloth, *The Fortunes of Father Mockinpott*, which appeared in 1976, also in the *Mainichi Daily News*.

I strove to see every Japanese classic film that had been made, as well as every new one. I particularly remember *Funeral Parade of Roses*, the 1969 film directed by Matsumoto Toshio. It was showing at the old Mimatsu Theater just northwest of the Shijo-Kawaramachi corner in downtown Kyoto. This movie gave a young Japanese actor by the single name of Peter a start to his career, and is a foundational film in the annals of gay cinema. (In the mid-1990s I became a colleague of Matsumoto Toshio at Kyoto University of Art and Design and got to know him well.)

One thing I loved about the old Mimatsu Theater was that it had a public bathhouse in the same building, so you could see a movie and soak in a hot tub after. Luxurious! I was and still am crazy about Japanese public baths. I went to them at least once a week while living in Tokyo. I am especially fond of the murals of Mt. Fuji or the Seto Inland Sea that many of these bathhouses have, and even contemplated writing a book about the unsung genre of bathhouse art.

I became a captive of the contemporary Japanese theater. I had not seen all that much theater before arriving in Japan. Two astounding productions, however, stood out in my mind. The first was John Gielgud's *Hamlet* on Broadway in 1964. My uncle Joe in New York had bought me a front-row seat; and I will never forget seeing Richard Burton, then still a young man and a superb actor, as Hamlet. This was the year he married Elizabeth Taylor (for the first time). The second production was that of *The Constant Prince* at Jerzy Grotowski's theater in Wroclaw in October 1966. I was so stunned by Grotowski's ensemble's performances that I was unable to get out of my seat at the end, causing me to miss the last train to Warsaw and forcing me to spend a shudderingly cold night on a platform bench at Wroclaw Station. (In April 2019 I revisited Wroclaw for the first time in fifty-three years at the invitation of the Grotowski Institute. It was so wonderful to be able to talk there about that ground-breaking production, as well as about Grotowski's visit to Australia in 1974 and the symposium we held in his honor in Tokyo in the year of his death, 1999.)

Dramatic things were happening in Japanese theater in the 1960s. The socalled Angura (Underground) Theater Movement had begun, and it was proving very popular with young people, who were in a phase of rebellion that the country has not seen since. Angura was also called the Shogekijo Undo, or Little Theater Movement, because most of the plays were performed at small venues. Among the exceptional productions I saw were plays by Betsuyaku Minoru, especially *The Elephant*, his brilliant study of the post-Hiroshima trauma as it affected the population there. I eventually translated *The Elephant*, which was produced in 1974 at the Mercury Theatre in Auckland, the largest theater in New Zealand, with the great Maori actor George Henare in the lead. I went to both Kara Juro's (Red Tent) Situation Theater when he pitched the big red tent by the grounds of the grand shrine at Shimogamo in Kyoto, and the Black Tent Theatre, where innovative and iconoclastic plays by Saito Ren, Sato Makoto and others were performed. I saw Inoue Hisashi's plays and remember being bowled over by his biting satire on Japanese life, *The Adventures of Dogen*. And there was Suzuki Tadashi's production of *In Search of the Theatrical*, a play that introduced the amazing female actor Shiraishi Kayoko.

At the forefront, as far as theater was concerned, stood Terayama Shuji, whose plays were enjoying recognition in Europe. In early 1970 I went up to Tokyo from Kyoto to his Tenjo Sajiki Theater in Shibuya with its bizarre collage façade inspired by artist Yotsuya Shimon. Fifteen years later a photograph of one of Shimon's lifesize dolls adorned the cover of my Japanese book about the theater and film renaissance of the 1960s, *Roger Pulvers's Showa Dramatic*.

The play that I saw at Terayama's space in Shibuya changed my life. (I also met Terayama there, as well as his infamous mother. But I only met him twice after that, and, I am sorry to say, we never became friends.) The play I saw was *The Crimes of Doctor Garigari*, the title being a pun on the title of the expressionist silent film classic of 1920, *The Cabinet of Dr. Caligari*. (*Garigari* is a mimetic word suggesting a grating sound.) Though I had never contemplated writing a play, this experience in Shibuya prompted me to do just that; and my little debut piece of theater was published in Japan's leading drama magazine, *Shingeki*, in August 1970 under the title, *The Perfect Crimes of Mrs. Garigari*. The action of the play, which thankfully has never seen the light of a stage, takes place when the cosmetic counter in a Japanese department store is hijacked by a radical foreign feminist. The idea was good; the execution, miserable.

Not even the avant-garde theater was enough for my insatiable curiosity about Japan. I had heard *naniwabushi* being performed on the radio, and without knowing much about it, I sought out a teacher who would teach me how to "grunt out" (*unaru*) these one-person dramatic ballads. My search took me to downtown Osaka, to the door of a little rundown office that was promoting naniwabushi. I hadn't realized that naniwabushi was in severe decline in Japan.

The people at the office welcomed me with open arms. The man was none other than the great master of Kansai naniwabushi, Tsukuba Musashi; the woman, his wife, Chikuba Musashi, who asked me to call her "Lady Musashi." They were very kind to me—after all, there had apparently never been a foreigner who wanted to perform naniwabushi; and after some months of study I was to become "Roger Musashi."

As a result, I commuted once a week from Midorogaike in northern Kyoto all the way to the south of Osaka at Kawachi Amami, where the Musashis lived, and learned what is called *isseki* (literally "one sitting," a performance of approximately thirty minutes) of the story of the Edo-period Japanese ruffian-hero, Nogitsune Sanji. It wasn't long before I was traveling around nursing homes in the Kansai region together with the Musashis (Lady Musashi played the shamisen), grunting and groaning it out as much as my vocal chords could stand. On March 28, 1972, I performed isseki of *Nogitsune Sanji* at the downtown Osaka Ward Auditorium in Abeno, a working-class district of the city. I had told some of my Sandai students about the performance, and they had promised they would come. But they didn't show up.

"Where were you?" I asked them the next day in class. "I looked for you in the audience."

"Oh, sir, we went to Abeno, but we saw it was naniwabushi, so we turned back. We thought you were doing *rakugo*." (Rakugo was, and still is, a much more popular form of one-person dramatic performance than naniwabushi. Naniwabushi performers sang the praises of the nation during the war, and the genre never recovered from the association with imperial policy.)

Through the naniwabushi connection, I was fortunate to meet many traveling performers who were still playing the local traps around Japan, as well as great naniwabushi performers like Baichuken Odo and Futaba Yuriko. (Naniwabushi had been open to women virtually since its inception as a performance art form in the Meiji era, and Futaba Yuriko was the foremost performer of it at the time.) I once went on TV with actor and promoter of traditional performance art Ozawa Shoichi, whom I was to meet many times later at Inoue Hisashi's home in Ichikawa, grunting out some naniwabushi in a duet with him. These days I don't grunt anymore, not even in the public baths, where, in the old days, it wasn't rare to hear the guttural strains of such old-fashioned balladeering cleaving the steam.

In early 1972 I was lucky enough to be one of the winners in a *Mainichi Shinbun* essay contest with an essay about Miyazawa Kenji. This link with the *Mainichi* was to prove crucial, for ten years later I went to work fulltime for its English-language edition, the *Mainichi Daily News*. It also gave me the chance to participate in a symposium with one of my favorite writers, Nosaka Akiyuki. NHK had also asked me to play the part of Mr. Higgins in their radio adaptation of Nosaka's short story, "Amerika Hijiki." "Amerika Hijiki" tells the story of a Japanese man with an inferiority complex toward Americans acquired during the Allied Occupation. He feels that he is harboring an American inside him to whom he must be subservient. For me, being an American with a Japanese inside him, this was a drama I was delighted to be a part of.

But then the unpredicted happened. I received a letter from a professor at the Australian National University in Canberra. He was coming to Kyoto and wished to meet. After the meeting, he offered me a job teaching Japanese language and literature in Canberra, a language and a literature that less than five years earlier I had known nothing about.

I said yes. But why? Why leave the Japan that I loved so much?

I had begun to write plays, thanks to the inspiration of Terayama, Inoue and Kara, but was unable to get any of them produced. I thought that if I went to Australia, there were bound to be theaters there and hopefully I could become a playwright. Or, I could always make a U-turn back to the northern hemisphere and return to Japan. I knew as little about Australia as I had about Japan before going there. It was a country that I had never contemplated moving to. Please recall that this was the era of the White Australia Policy, before the renaissance in Australian film and the charm offensive of Australian culture around the world. Australia was not a popular destination for Japanese at the time either. But I have always asked myself "Why not?" rather than "Why?" I was only twenty-eight.

My Norwegian wife was interested in going to Australia too. We had no children whose welfare to consider.

It was the unknown that beckoned again, the bend in the road where you could not see around the corner, when you didn't know where you were headed, when you were disoriented, in a place where you knew no one and no one knew you. That was the kind of place I wanted to be.

So, in August 1972, I quit Kyoto Sangyo University and flew down to the southern hemisphere and into the unknown. The result was to be a new career, a new citizenship, a new wife and four children born to us.

But whatever would be my life in Australia, I always knew that Japan was my real home, and the complete imperfection in culture the pinnacle of what I hoped, in a very small way, to create on my own.

5

THE FIVE JAPANS

And so I left my beloved Kyoto, with its deep muddy pond, on the night of August 13, 1972. The next time I was to look up, to the beautiful clear night sky of Canberra, Orion the Hunter was standing on his head, and there were celestial objects and stars, including the Magellanic Clouds and the Southern Cross, that I had never seen before. I felt as if I had taken the same route as Giovanni and Campanella on Kenji's Milky Way Train, southward on the River of the Sky.

Some six months earlier, on February 2 to be exact, sergeant in the Imperial Japanese Army Yokoi Shoichi had returned to Japan for the first time since the war. When he hobbled down the stairs from the airplane onto the tarmac, he was seated in a wheelchair and an object was thrust in his hand. He waved this object in the air, showing all his teeth in a big smile. Does anyone reading this book recall what that object was? It was a symbol of the new Japan. What single small object do you think symbolized Japan in 1972? It was something unimaginable to a person who had been isolated from his country for three decades.

It was, in fact, a 10,000-yen note. Ten thousand yen would have been a fortune to someone before the war. Now it was the symbol of everything that Yokoi Shoichi's country had achieved since his "disappearance" on Guam. I watched this on television with a keen sense of regret. People in the United States were beginning to call the Japanese "economic animals." I never accepted the validity of this term. If anyone it was the Americans, with their obsessively materialistic lifestyle, who were the economic animals. But, could there be some truth to what they were saying about the Japanese; or was it merely a label applied to them to debunk the "miracle" of rebirth, recovery and a rapid rate of growth that threatened the hegemony of the United States, just as China's does today?

It was the era of the wildly popular *nihonjinron*, or theories about the Japanese national character, the three best known being Nakane Chie's *Japanese Society*, Doi Takeo's *The Anatomy of Dependence*, and a book that I thought as suspicious in origin as it was superficial in analysis, *The Japanese and the Jews*, by an author who called himself Isaiah Ben-Dasan. (I knew from the outset that it had been written by a Japanese using a Jewish nom de plume). Both Nakane's and Doi's books depicted the Japanese people as living in highly structured formal relationships to each other based on social hierarchies. This fit the postwar Western stereotype of the Japanese people; and Western adulation for those two books in turn fed Japanese interest. The Japanese were eager to analyze themselves and intrigued more than ever about how the outside world viewed them. When I was interviewed about Japan and the Japanese, the phrase "blue-eyed" (a cliché used to described Western foreigners) was often used to sum up my viewpoint, even though my eyes are dark brown and I was striving constantly to observe Japan from the inside. Few Japanese at the time were themselves liberated enough to consider this so much as a possibility. If you said something original, it was seen as quirky, exotic and largely inaccurate. If you repeated the obvious, you might just be praised for "understanding us so well." There was no inhabitable territory in between.

Let's look once again at the title of Nakane Chie's bestselling book, that is, the Japanese title. Not at the title actually, but rather at the subtitle and a particular word in it. The original subtitle was *Tan'itsu Shakai no Riron* (A Theory on a Homogeneous Society). The word tan'itsu, or homogeneous, became quite popular after that, especially in the phrase "tan'itsu minzoku," a homogeneous people. By using this term, the Japanese people nurtured a notion of themselves as ethnically homogeneous, which they most certainly are not.

Now, a view of your nation as being ethnically homogeneous is one that may facilitate rapid growth. All for one and one for all. The

THE FIVE JAPANS

peg that sticks out will be battered down, as the modern take on the old Japanese proverb goes. (The original meaning of this proverb was closer to "A chain is only as strong as its weakest link," not quite the same as one indicating blanket conformity.) This is the perfect ethic for a country rebuilding its pride after an ignominious defeat and the total devastation of cities and towns. So it was natural after the war, and perhaps even economically desirable, that Japanese people viewed themselves in this uniform light, despite the blatant untruth of the concept of ethnic homogeneity.

I had just spent five years in a country whose culture I saw as one with a stunning variety in every aspect of life: ways of thinking and acting and talking, senses of humor, food, art, music, you-name-it. Why was everyone, both inside and outside Japan, subscribing to the view that these people were ethnically homogeneous when they obviously were not?

I came to formulate a theory to reflect the cultural reality of the Japanese nation, a theory which I called "The Five Japans." Each one of these Japans was different in so many ways from the other, and yet they were all representative of the country and its people. And what of Japanese literature? What did Miyazawa Kenji and Kawabata Yasunari have in common? Or the decadent Sakaguchi Ango and the revanchist Mishima Yukio? They had only one thing in common: They all wrote in Japanese. And it wasn't even a similar style of Japanese in any way. What did the design and color sensibilities of classic shibui (understated) craft have in common with those of Okinawa? I never bought the homogeneous Japan myth, not then, back in the early seventies, and not now.

What are the Five Japans? Needless to say, there are other regions and districts of Japan with unique cultural features, and there are also wide ethnic variations within each of these broad categories. There are even stark differences in the customs, dialects, arts and cuisines among the six prefectures of Tohoku.

The Five Japans represent a simplified categorization of Japanese culture.

They are …

Tohoku
Tokyo (Edo)
Kyoto-Nara (Yamato)
Kitakyushu
Okinawa

It dawned on me when, in the summer and autumn of 1977, I was staying at Inoue Hisashi's home in Ichikawa. I woke up one day and did something I had never done before. Impetuously I packed a little bag, rushed to Tokyo Station and bought a train ticket for Akita, the only prefecture in Tohoku that I had not been to.

Why did I do this? I didn't know at the time but I was suffering, for the only time in my life, from a mild case of nervous exhaustion. I had left Australia in May of that year, flying directly from Canberra to Stockholm, Sweden, a thirty-three-hour-long journey. In Stockholm I was one of two Australian representatives at the International Theater Institute (ITI) convention. From Stockholm I went to Oslo, where I met up with my wife, and from there I went alone to Warsaw at the invitation of the Polish Authors' Agency. I spent a month in Warsaw translating a new play for them and seeing old friends like film director Andrzej Wajda, whom I had met the Expo '70 in Osaka and whose country house I had stayed at in the summer of 1970. Andrzej lived in an old manor house between Warsaw and Lublin. The house was the birthplace of the great nineteenth-century Polish poet, Cyprian Norwid.

My wife joined me in Warsaw and we flew together to Tokyo. We were met at the airport by Hisashi's wife Yoshiko, who drove us to their home in Ichikawa. I hadn't yet realized that my marriage was standing on shaky ground. There was certainly some love and a good deal of mutual admiration left in it. But somehow I was beginning to feel, subconsciously, that this was not happiness. Eventually we divorced and I married Susan, my wife now of thirty-seven years and the mother of our four children.

Life in Tokyo was hectic. I was writing my first novel, *The Death of Urashima Taro*, and producing several articles a week for the *Mainichi Daily News* and a host of other publications, both English-language and Japanese-language, as well as translating Hisashi's prose. This activity, combined with my inner unhappiness in marriage, was taking a toll on my nerves that I was unaware of.

I impulsively set out for Akita, arrived in the city and checked into a little inn. The next morning I stood by the side of the road outside the city and was picked up by some fishermen who were driving around the Oga Peninsula. I tell you, I didn't understand a single word of what they said in their thick Akita dialect. For a moment, I suspected they were speaking Korean. We stopped along the shoreline and the fishermen produced a huge plastic bucket of salmon roe and a jumbo bottle of sake—I don't recall the brand or even if it had a brand—from the back of the truck. The three of us devoured the roe with large soupspoons and drank sake out of plastic cups, conversing for about an hour. I say "conversing" but all I could do was say, "Uh-huh ... oh ... well, yes, I suppose so ..." and "I see." I said "I see," but I didn't see a thing and hadn't a clue as to what they were talking about. As for them, they probably hadn't expected a foreigner to understand Japanese anyway.

I returned from Akita to Tokyo with my confidence shattered. I would never really understand the culture of Akita without learning the dialect. And the same went for Aomori, Iwate and the other prefectures of Tohoku.

The prefecture in Tohoku that I came to know the best was Iwate. Iwate had produced, as contemporaries, tanka poet Ishikawa Takuboku and Miyazawa Kenji. (A tanka, with its thirty-one syllables, is a "long haiku.") As for Takuboku, I have translated many of his tanka. His short life (twenty-six years) was fascinating, full of conflicting romances, travel and insightful commentary. He was also that rare bird in today's terms: a socially committed leftwing popular author. He looked with a jaundiced eye on the face of his people ...

Its features
Are too coarse for words.
I choose to stay home.

A self-deprecating irony permeates his work. Does he stay at home because he cannot bear to look upon other Japanese faces or because he does not want to show his own?

I often wrote in my weekly *Japan Times* column, "Counterpoint," a column I maintained for the eight years, that young people of today should take inspiration from their native Japanese culture. Well, Takuboku is just what the doctor ordered.

One of Japan's greatest and most innovative poets, Takuboku underwent a personal awakening from plaintive romantic to keen radical. His transformation can serve as an example to rouse today's introverted young people to active awareness of their nation's "dilemma of disconnectedness" with their cultural past.

Takuboku was revolted by the apathy on the part of ordinary Japanese to injustices so blatant before their eyes; at the deterioration of their freedoms that they seemed to accept without resistance. He was particularly incensed by the indifference of people to the fate of Kotoku Shusui, the eminent Japanese intellectual socialist who was executed for treason along with others on trumped-up charges on January 24, 1911. Restless, introspective and distressed by public lassitude, Takuboku, who died April 13, 1912, speaks for all youth, all over the world, now.

As for Miyazawa Kenji, no other place except Iwate has produced such a genius in literature, science and religious thought. Kenji's view of man as only one part of all creation, as a single light that can continue to shine even after the body is gone ("the lamp itself is lost"), bringing happiness to other humans, other animals and all nature, is vitally necessary to the world today. I see Kenji's philosophy as coming not so much out of Japan as specifically out of Iwate. The wild and enthralling landscape—what Kenji called the "lightscape"—of Iwate is the stage, the illumination and the sound system for this world-class wordsmith. His poetry is so much about light that he observed himself as indistinguishable from it ...

*The phenomenon called I
Is a single blue illumination
Of a presupposed organic alternating current lamp ...
  (the light is preserved ... the lamp itself is lost)*

In the unique cultures of Tohoku we also find sadsack novelist Dazai Osamu from Tsugaru in Aomori prefecture. His popularity seems to be as strong in Japan today as it ever was. There are the folktales of Tono, retold by folklorist/ethnographer Yanagita Kunio. (I lived not far away from his son's home in Seijo, and used to make a detour to the station in order to see the eucalyptus tree— symbolically Australia's national tree—that Yanagita himself had planted in his garden in 1943, no doubt from a seedling that came from South-East Asia or the South Pacific under Japanese rule at the time. Yanagita's daughter-in-law told me that it was the first eucalyptus planted in Tokyo.)

Tohoku occupies a bizarre presence in Japan. The landscape is the thing that is most important in all Japanese aesthetics, and the landscape of Tohoku is full of variety and spectacular manifestations in its mountains, waterfalls, coastline, and in its extreme climate and catastrophic seismic disorder. At the same time Tohoku boasts an absolute serenity in the placid Oirase Valley.

Tohoku is certainly one very distinct and different Japan in look, in sensation, in ethnic and cultural import.

The second Japan is Edo: chic, sharp, brash and cool Tokyo.

The culture of Tokyo is a kind of "pilfered culture," pilfered and amalgamated from many parts of the country. As such it represents the coming together of contemporary Japanese culture. Virtually all the cultural organizations and organs, such as publishers, theaters, etc., are concentrated in this city. Everywhere else is called the *chiho*, or provinces, and one cannot deny a slight sense of condescension in this usage. If New Yorkers called Chicago or San Francisco the provinces, people in those cities would declare war on the city! (New York alone does retain a Tokyo-style cultural snobbishness. For years shows would have a "provincial opening" before the "real thing" came to Broadway.) I doubt that there is any other capital in the developed world where the control over the culture of the country is so concentrated in one place as it is in Tokyo.

Tokyo culture is like the B-grade-gourmet dish *oyakodonburi*. You take a little bit of rice, which is the substance of all Japanese culture, you toss together a mixture of chicken bits, onion and half-cooked egg, and plonk it on top of the rice. The top part never really mixes with the bottom, making Tokyo culture an eternally unamalgamated culture. But the half-cooked egg somehow goes slipping and sliding down through the rice to give it flavor and, together with the soy-based sauce, unifies the whole and somehow makes sense. Tokyo culture is definitely thrown together and best consumed fast, like oyakodonburi.

Anything goes in Tokyo. Tokyo produces a Horiguchi Daigaku, poet and translator from French who was born where it counts, in Hongo, home of schools and universities; and it also produces flashy entrepreneur Horiemon (Horie Takafumi), who was born in Fukuoka but went to the prestigious Tokyo University (until he dropped out). There was a time when the delicate and exquisite culture of Kyoto represented Japan in the world. Now it is Tokyo, for better or worse, that speaks for Japan, in the four-faceted MASK phenomenon, in fashion and in every other aspect of Japanese life. Tokyo culture is cosmopolitan and in some ways more like the culture of New York, Paris and Sydney than it is like that of Morioka, Yamagata or Aomori, three major cities in Tohoku.

Tokyo culture may represent Japan today, but to me it is only one of the many cultures of the nation.

The third Japan is that of Kyoto-Nara, referred to by its old name, Yamato. Kyoto sits in a basin, and the appearance from the city is that you are surrounded on three sides by hills with elegant curves. Being an inland basin, the winters are cold and the summers are exceedingly hot and humid. Once you have lived in Kyoto, you can live just about anywhere else in Japan (except some parts of Tohoku, perhaps, where the snowfall is the highest in the world for an inhabited area).

The entire Heian period (794-1185) culture is embroidered from the threads of Kyoto's elegant and subtle aesthetics. This includes, of course, Murasaki Shikibu's *The Tale of Genji* and a book I prefer, *The Pillow Book of Sei Shonagon*. The many hundreds of amazing temples and shrines, with their distinct architecture, statues and gardens; the noh, kyogen and kabuki; the tea ceremony—they all originated or flourished in Kyoto, though, as I have written in connection with noh, they draw on sources that come from other parts of Asia. Even some noh masks originate in their expression from outside Japan. Old man Okina is, in essence, a Korean mask. And Beshimi, that ferocious looking mask with its wide nose, has a distinctly Indian face and coloring. Even noh, considered by many Japanese to be the "purest" form of Japanese performance, is neither ethnically Japanese in origin nor artistically homogeneous in gesture and movement.

I went to the noh theater often in Kyoto, and, whenever I could, also attended bugaku and gagaku performances, both traditional music and dance art forms originating in China. I loved going to see Mibu Kyogen every year at Mibudera, a temple in Kyoto. Mibu Kyogen is one of the forms of this comic dramatic genre that is truly comic. I went to Nara for Omizutori, the "water-drawing festival" in which the night is set alight and noh is performed in the glare of torches. Both of these festivals have their origins in Asian continental ritual. Everywhere you go there are reminders of the Japanese past as a cosmopolitan Asian culture.

The Yamato culture that originated in Nara and Kyoto is the culture of Buddhist thought, of contemplation, of a deeply aesthetic religiosity and an equally deeply aesthetic eroticism. There are five noh plays about Ono-no-Komachi, whose beauty and wit remain legendary today. Tokyo culture is brash male culture; Kyoto culture, soft, sensuous and thrilling female culture. The culture of Yamato is, in essence, simplicity itself. Sen no Rikyu, the illustrious tea master of the sixteenth century, wrote, "The Way of Tea is no more than boiling water, making tea and drinking it." Despite the surface intricacy of the Yamato culture, the ideal is still to come full circle back to everything pure, simple and "as is."

I frequented the old Kagetsu Theater on Shinkyogoku Street in downtown Kyoto, reopened in recent years at a new location after being closed for many years. There you could see Japanese performance arts such as naniwabushi, *manzai* (a two-person comic routine), *kodan* (one of the many arts of dramatic recitation), skits, magic and other wonderful traditional and modern performance arts. Kyoto culture had its less elegant side too. When German architect Bruno Taut praised the wonders of Kyoto's Katsura Detached Palace as the epitome of Japanese aesthetics, author and unreconstructed iconoclast Sakaguchi Ango countered by saying, "If he wanted to see Kyoto culture he should go to the toilets at the Arashiyama Theater. Japanese culture reeks of urine."

The fourth Japan is Kitakyushu, or northern Kyushu.

No doubt the influence of Korean culture on Yamato had been significant in every aspect of aesthetic life. (Nara, Japan's ancient capital, means "country" in Korean.) But when I traveled around Kitakyushu, I felt I was actually back in Korea itself. The influence of Korean culture on the Japanese aesthetic cannot be overestimated, something many Japanese are reluctant to admit, preferring, rather, to ascribe the influences to China.

There was, as I wrote, the pottery of Onta and Koishiwara. But Korean influences on Kyushu ceramics spread from Oita in the north, through Karatsu and Arita in Saga prefecture and down to Kagoshima in the south. The little Buddhist statues by the sides of the roads in the Kunisaki Peninsula in Oita; the five hundred statues of the *rakan*, or disciples, near Usa, each with an individual expression—it all looked so continental to me, rather than "Japanese." But it was and is Japan, a Japan whose culture was inspired by neighbors just across the channel. Koreans are the cultural older cousins of the Japanese.

It is no wonder that Fukuoka in northern Kyushu sees itself as a cultural bridge between Japan and Korea, and is host of a huge Asian film festival. Wouldn't it be wonderful if every child in

Kyushu studied Korean in school, to help them understand the roots of their culture?

The fifth Japan, Okinawa, is one that I hadn't appreciated until I first went there at the end of 1977. From Naha my first wife and I flew to the island of Ishigaki and then took a boat to the jungle-covered island of Iriomote. From there we hired a small boat for the thirty-minute (and very rough) crossing to Hatoma, where we spent four weeks. She made an ethnographic film on the island, one which now is a very precious resource, I believe, of Yaeyama culture at the time, and I typed out the handwritten manuscript of *The Death of Urashima Taro* on the portable Brother typewriter I had brought there. This was to become my first published novel in Japanese and English.

There was no water on Hatoma at the time and it had to be pumped from Iriomote through an undersea pipe. We swam every day in the island's beautiful bays, for though it was late December to early January, the days there, just a degree above the tropics, are warm and pleasant. We ate bonito caught nearby (there was an old disused smoked bonito-shaving plant on the island) and ray fins in soup. Less than fifty people lived on Hatoma at the time, and we met most of them.

Solrun was making her film, and I was typing my novel. Though I helped her with her filming from time to time, and though we didn't argue, I wouldn't say that our marriage was a happy one. That year, 1978, we returned to Australia, flying from Naha to Manila (Northwest Airlines flew that route in those days; it was a hangover from the time of the Allied Occupation) and on to Australia. It was the year I meet Susan and fell head over heels in love with her.

Before then, when we were still in Naha on the main island of Okinawa, I had noticed something very different from all other parts of Japan. We were invited to a person's home. The wife brought out some food and offered it to us.

"Oh, no, thank you very much, but I couldn't," I said, bowing my head and sucking in air through my mouth. I was acting in my normal way for that time, which was very much like your standard, formal and stiff Japanese.

The lady was surprised.

"What? Don't you want it? I made this, so it's good," she said.

I had never heard these words from a Japanese host or hostess. Food was always served with self-deprecating phrases of how hopeless a cook the person was or, at best, "It might not taste good to you, but please do try it."

Here was a Japan that was unlike the customary one I had come to know. Some people in Kyoto are especially insulted if a guest actually takes wagashi, or tea cakes, that have been offered. It is etiquette to refuse to take offered food in some Kyoto circles. Okinawan hospitality could not have been more different.

The people of Okinawa and the southernmost Japanese islands of Yaeyama were outgoing and instinctively friendly, not reserved and standoffish like so many Japanese people are in public. And their culture of music was far more full of joy, it seemed to me, than that of the other Japans I had known (except for the raucous Tsugaru shamisen up in Tohoku). Their color sense was also different. I particularly fell for the *Yaeyama jofu* style in textiles, one characterized by a fine weave of hemp with splashed patterns. One design template features a recurring pattern of five and four rectangles. This works as an abstract design. But it also signifies something romantic in the Yaeyama personality. Five can be read *itsu*, and four, *yo*. *Itsu no yo made* means "forever and ever."

This phrase came to take on a special meaning when I wrote my novel *Star Sand* in Japanese and English, and later when I adapted it for the screen and directed it. The heroine, Hiromi, gives the American deserter Bob a thin obi adorned with this romantic pattern.

Another discovery on Hatoma became the key itself to the *Star Sand* story. The beaches and seabed surrounding the isle are made up not of sand but in countless tiny star-like protozoa carcasses known as *hoshizuna*, or star sand. These little creatures, long dead, came to symbolize for me the link between the earth and the sky. In the film, Bob flings a handful of star sand into the sky, then tells

Hiromi that it will stay there "forever and ever" and always be a link between all people, wherever they are.

In southern Okinawa I saw vestiges of the cultures of China, Polynesia and Southeast Asia. Japan is indeed linked to places far beyond its shores.

What variety and richness there is in Japan! And how it all seems lost when we think of those limited theories of homogeneity of decades past, where all Japanese were said to be similar in manner and custom, a nation of attaché-case conformists.

No sentence that begins "The Japanese are" can be correct about this country unless its speaker or author recognizes the sophisticated traditions and myriad customs that came to form the pluralistic essence of this cultural melting pot called Japan.

6

MIRACULOUS MOMENTS

How did I end up in Australia? It was all because of the Second World War.

A world war affects not only the hundreds of millions of people living through it at the time, but many more hundreds of millions of people of subsequent generations. War is a gargantuan ugly and misshapen ship creating mountain-high waves on all sides, waves that inundate villages, towns and cities, destroying life and property on a massive scale. As with a ship, war stirs up a wake that continues to sway the lives of the people long after its physical presence has vanished beyond the horizon.

The wake created by Warship World War II had a sway on my life too, though I was barely a year old when it ended. I found myself one day on the shores of Australia. This is how is happened.

As 1971 was drawing to a close, I received a letter out of the blue from a professor at the Australian National University in Canberra, Sydney Crawcour. He wrote that he had heard about me, was coming to Kyoto and would like to have a talk. I set up a meeting at the information counter in Takashimaya department store on the corner of Shijo-Kawaramachi. After we met, I took him to an *unagi* (eel) restaurant on Hanamikoji Street in Gion. (Unagi and *hamo*, the large conger eel, are Kyoto specialties.)

Before we finished the meal, Professor Crawcour offered me a job at the ANU, an institution I had never heard of before receiving his letter. As for where Canberra was, what kind of a culture Australia had, what the landscape looked like or anything else about the country, I was just as ignorant as I had once been about Japan, perhaps more so.

It wasn't until I had settled in Canberra and had been teaching for some months that I learned how Professor Crawcour had come to contact me.

During the war, Sydney Crawcour had been a young officer in the Australian armed forces. The end of the war found him looking after Japanese POWs awaiting repatriation. The POWs, all being ex-soldiers, were disciplined by their own officers. It goes without saying that once having surrendered, the Japanese soldiers were admirably cooperative and well behaved.

Sydney Crawcour had become friends with an officer in charge of POW camp discipline. Not long after that, all of the soldiers and officers were repatriated. As for Sydney Crawcour, he decided to study Japanese language and economics, becoming one of Australia's foremost experts on Japan. He also maintained contact with the ex-officer, who had returned to Osaka and become a successful businessman.

In 1971, Professor Crawcour was paying a visit to his old friend (and enemy) in Osaka when he mentioned that he was looking for a new teacher at the ANU, someone who was fluent in Japanese and could teach a course in modern Japanese literature. It just so happened that the man's son was a student of mine at the university.

"My teacher at Sandai is really good at Japanese," said the student. "He really loves Japanese literature, too."

So it is thanks to my ex-student and the fact that his father had been a POW that I ended up in Australia, met Susan and had four children. Yes, many things happen in the wake of a war, some of them, as years pass, turning into peaceful ripples.

Did I *decide* to go to Australia? No. It was decided for me by circumstances. I can tell you why I prefer one cheese over another or why I went to a museum yesterday instead of to the cinema. I had knowledge of the alternatives—be they a variety of cheese, the art on exhibit or the particular movies playing at the time. But in the very biggest decisions that we make in life—where we live and work, who we marry—we may have much less choice than we believe. We are merely presented with some circumstance and that becomes our fate. That is why I have written here that I "ended up" in Australia. That is where I happened to come to be.

Later I fell hopelessly in love with Susan, and thanks to her now have four grown children. But did I choose to fall in love with her? I don't think so. The famous Pushkin love poem tells it all in two of its lines ...

I recall a miraculous moment
When, before me, you appeared

That's it: a miraculous moment. The momentous events in our lives are brought about and ruled by just such miraculous moments. An Australian officer talks to a Japanese through the wire fence of a POW camp in 1945 ... a biologist from Liverpool (Susan's father) decides to emigrate to Canberra to teach at the Australian National University in 1960 ... and in 1983, 1984, 1986 and 1989 four children are born to parents who would never have met had it not been for a series of miraculous moments, some of them occurring before any of us were born.

In Australia I found myself disoriented once again, under stars I didn't know the names of, in a country that was dry (Japan is wet), generally flat in most places (Japan is mountainous in most places) and bathed by the clearest and sharpest light (Japan is haze and mist and fog).

Even though I was to participate fully in Australian culture as novelist, playwright, theater director, translator, journalist and broadcaster; and even though I was, on July 6, 1976, to forfeit my American citizenship and become an Australian, I still considered Japan my home. (I had wished that my application for Australian citizenship could have been approved just two days earlier, the bicentennial of the Declaration of Independence.)

As I walked along bright Canberra streets—so bright, as Kenji wrote about one of his days, that "even the air hurts when you look"—I still carried Japan inside me and sang that most popular Japanese song softly to myself, a song whose words never fail to bring tears to my eyes.

Was it then I caught sight of you?
Am I dreaming this?
Gathering wild mulberries
In that little basket ...

Every Japanese person will immediately recognize the words of the song that the NHK show *Nihon no Uta, Furusato no Uta* (*Songs of Japan, Songs of Our Hometowns*) found in a nationwide survey in 1989 to be the favorite song of the nation: "Akatonbo," or "Red Dragonfly."

I get all choked up when I hear this song not only for love of its symbol, the red dragonfly. The song's sentimentality is magnified for me because of the life story of the author of its lyrics, Miki Rofu.

To Rofu (he, like Kenji, is referred to by his given name in Japan), the gathering of wild mulberries was a task associated with his mother. Even when he patiently waited, counting the berries, she did not come home. The fact is that Rofu's mother left home when he was five and never returned. His longing for her, as expressed most tenderly in "Akatonbo," preoccupied him for his entire life. (I wish people in foreign countries would sing this song and learn about Rofu's life. Then they would see what a sentimental and emotional people the Japanese are!)

Rofu's father was the profligate scion of wealth in Tatsuno, Hyogo prefecture, a small town on the Seto Inland Sea so lovely it was called "little Kyoto." His mother, Kata, who was married off at age fifteen, gave birth to two boys, Misao (Rofu) and Tsutomu. But she soon tired of her husband disappearing (or, to use the Japanese word, "evaporating") on alcoholic binges.

In 1895, when Rofu was five, his parents divorced, and Kata, with two-year-old Tsutomu on her back, departed for her hometown of Tottori. Rofu returned home from kindergarten one day and his mother was simply not there. (The story of Midorikawa Kata's life as magazine editor and early feminist in Hokkaido deserves a book in itself.) It wasn't until he was eighteen that Rofu received a letter from his mother, who was then living in the northern Hokkaido town of Otaru. It is said that he clutched the letter to him and wept uncontrollably.

Midorikawa Kata died in 1962, at the age of ninety-one. Carved on her white marble gravestone are the words "At rest here, little dragonfly's mother."

As for Rofu himself, he died only two years later, age seventy-five. He was leaving a post office in Mitaka, Tokyo, was struck by a taxi and rushed to hospital, where he was pronounced dead. The most poignant lines of his song are the final ones, conjuring an image of naïve and solitary beauty ...

At sunset and in the twilight's glow
Little red dragonfly
Resting, waiting
On the end of a bamboo pole

These beautiful lines of Japanese poetry were ones he had written seven years after his mother left home, when he was twelve.

Forgive me for spending so much time and space on a sentimental old song. But to me, Japanese culture is something that cannot be understood with the head. It must be absorbed through the pores of the skin and taken in as sound and color and textures. The visual texture of the lyrics of "Akatonbo"—particularly in the final image of the end of a bamboo pole, the kind used in the old days to hang out the wash—is quintessentially Japanese, as Japanese as *The Tale of Genji*, the tea ceremony, Basho's haiku that ends not with a red dragonfly at the end of a bamboo pole but with a frog splashing into the water, or Kawabata Yasunari's exquisite novel, *The Sound of the Mountain*.

Even though I was in Australia and had taken up Australian citizenship, the Japanese person inside me would always be inexpressibly drawn to the beauty and sadness of Miki Rofu's little red dragonfly. It was, and still is, more important to me than any passport could ever be.

Is it incongruous to be walking along a street in Australia on a hot and dry December day with the strains of "Akatonbo" going through your head over and over again? Not at all. We carry all of our experiences with us, like little tickets that line our pockets, sticking to the sides of them, never letting us forget that our lives are made up of a compilation of tickets and passes to a multitude of destinations.

So here was an American, who got all blubbery over a little red Japanese insect, becoming a citizen of a country, Australia, he had never even considered going to before receiving a single letter in the mail. I knew that if I did become an Australian, I would naturally inherit the nefarious deeds of my new country's past. Australia had been a cultural backwater. It was a country with a sustained history of prejudice against non-white people. It had participated willingly in the Vietnam War. After all, it was an Australian prime minister, Harold Holt, who gleefully took credit for coining the phrase "All the way with LBJ." You can't just absorb the good qualities of the country you throw your lot in with. Everything in its past becomes part of your new identity, the whole kit and caboodle.

Just as with the magic lantern in which I saw, on my first night in Japan, a world I wanted to absorb and make a part of me, so it was with Australia. It was a color that convinced me that, come what may, I was going to be Australian. That color was red. But not the bright red of lipstick, or the smoky red you see on Japanese shrine gates or the vermillion of Japanese inkpads. It was the reddish ochre of the Australian outback that became the true color of my Australian passport.

Again, Poland played a part in this new identity, another series of randomly assembled miraculous moments determining fate.

While living in Poland, I had become fascinated by the plays of Stanislaw Witkiewicz, who is today considered Poland's greatest playwright. Witkiewicz traveled to Australia in 1914 and wrote a play, *The Metaphysics of the Two-Headed Calf*, set in that country. It remains, to my knowledge, the only play written by a major European playwright set in Australia.

I translated the play in 1972 and a theater troupe asked for permission to perform it. This was no ordinary theater troupe in Sydney or Melbourne. It was the Alice Springs Theater Company, located, as the name suggests, smack in the middle of the continent, a place that Aussies call "the Red Centre." The other name for the company was the "Totem Theatre," a name that Witkiewicz, an aficionado of the occult, would have approved of.

This was the world premiere of this play in English, and I was eager to attend the performances. Luckily enough I was given a travel grant by the Australia Council for the Arts to fly to the Red Centre to see the production. The play was actually performed very professionally for an amateur troupe; and I suspect that Witkiewicz's ghost (there are lots of ghosts in his work) was pleased. Alice Springs in 1973 was not essentially different from the Australia he had witnessed in 1914.

I made a few short trips around the Red Centre, one to Ayers Rock, now called Uluru, as it should be. Uluru was returned to its rightful indigenous owners in 1985. When I got home to Canberra, I noticed that the white sneakers I had been wearing had been dyed the deep ochre red of the outback soil. Even after washing those sneakers in the washing machine, the color remained. I thought, "This color is indelible in me. I am going to live with it for the rest of my life."

In other words it was a combination of Witkiewicz's ghost, who led me to the Red Centre of Australia, and the red of the soil that caused me to sink into the life of my new country.

And how different it was from Japan! You couldn't get more different. Australia was empty; in Japan there are people wherever you go. Australia is all brash light and clarity; Japan is the country, in Tanizaki's phrase, that "glorifies shadow." The people whose European culture dominates Australia have been there for only two-hundred-odd years; Japan's culture is ancient and full of stories and myths going back millennia.

Productions of my plays started to go on in Melbourne, Canberra, Adelaide and other cities. I was writing for several national and local newspapers and magazines on a regular basis. I forged a career for myself in radio, reporting on cultural matters in Japan and Europe, and writing and narrating hour-long programs for the ABC, one about General MacArthur in Australia and another about Mishima Yukio. I even translated Nogitsune Sanji into English, changing that young raffish Edo hero into "Billy the Kid," and performed it in a cowboy uniform at the Nimrod Theatre, Sydney's most popular theater at the time. This was the first—and no doubt the last—performance of naniwabushi in Australia.

So, was my role to be a suspension bridge between two countries that I had come to love, neither of which was the one of my birth? Was I to be a frail little red dragonfly, flitting between one place and another, feeling at home in both but not truly accepted as a native in either? Australian culture was entering a phase of robust nationalism, and someone with an American accent, no matter how deep his identification with the cause, was viewed by many as a controlling intruder.

I traveled a good deal in the 1970s to many parts of Australia. I also went back to Poland to see my wonderful friend, film director Andrzej Wajda, whose life and work have been a constant inspiration to me. I took trips back to Paris, to Britain, Germany, Holland and Scandinavia. But the place that drew me every year was Japan; and I thought, when I was there as a visitor throughout the 1970s, "Someday I am going to return, to once again enter into the light of that magic lantern, that place where I feel most at home."

The 1960s had proved to be a pivotal decade for Japanese culture. It all began, as I see it, on June 15, 1960, the day University of Tokyo student Kanba Michiko was killed in a clash with riot police while demonstrating against the ANPO Treaty of Mutual Cooperation and Security between Japan and the United States. Young people today should be reminded that mass demonstrations, participated in not only by students but by ordinary citizens of every age, took place throughout the 1960s, reminding us all that the spirit of rebellion against politics forced on the people from above was once alive and kicking. This should tell us that the pervasive apathy and inertia we see in the Japanese populace today is not a fixed feature of the national character.

Postwar writing, in fiction and nonfiction, attacking cultural orthodoxy and establishment ways of thinking by such brilliant authors as Sakaguchi Ango and Oda Sakunosuke had created a spirit of rebellion that inspired the generation of Japanese who were young in the 1950s and '60s. Add to this the antiwar literature of Ooka Shohei, Takeda Taijun, Takeyama Michio and others like them, and you had a young generation who could not easily accept the pronouncements handed down to them as diktat by their reactionary government (whose prime minister, Kishi Nobusuke, was saved from being indicted as a war criminal by an American government that needed his "skills").

When I arrived in Japan in 1967, the underground culture in theater, film and the graphic arts was in full swing. The very next year, Oshima Nagisa made his outstanding film of the era, *Diary of a Shinjuku Thief*. Artist Yokoo Tadanori steals a book from a place at the center of Shinjuku culture, the Kinokuniya Bookstore, and this begins a story of restless rebellion. The film was brilliantly designed by one of the geniuses of Japanese cinema, Toda Jusho. (I write more about Toda Jusho and Oshima Nagisa in Chapter 8.) Playwright/director Kara Juro plays the guitar and sings in *Diary of a Shinjuku Thief* and Fua Mansaku, the wonderful actor I directed in the Japanese premiere of Sam Shepard's *Buried Child* at Parco Part 3 Theater in Shibuya, appears with other members of Kara's Situation Theater, including Kara's then-wife, Korean Japanese actress Li Reisen. Oshima's films of the 1960s comprise a spiritual guide to the astounding culture of that decade and how Japanese responded to it.

But the culture of 1960s Japan was halted in its march forward in February 1972, when the police laid siege to a mountain lodge, known as the Asama Sanso, in Karuizawa. This marked the end of the radical student movement, which, in any case, had fallen victim to its own inner struggles. This was followed in 1973 by the Oil Shock that rocked Japan into a sober reassessment of its place in the world. Once again the Japanese people were called upon to put their noses to the grindstone and work hard to ensure that the country continued to grow and prosper. There was no time left for restless rebellion and the culture that inspired it.

It goes without saying that cultural eras do not just click off and shut down like the rounded bar of a cheap lock that is pushed into its little hole. Kara Juro continued to write and present new plays in his red tent that toured the country. Oshima Nagisa made two of his best films about the ravages that war inflicts on the nation's conscience, *The Ceremony* in 1971 and *In the Realm of the Senses* in 1976. For the latter, the film was sent to France for processing to avoid the kind of censorship that the Japanese film industry was compelled to work under in Japan at the time.

The emergence of another major voice in theater in the 1970s, that of Korean Japanese playwright Tsuka Kohei, testifies to the fact that cultural eras do not come as gifts to the nation in neat little ten-year packages. There is—as there is with generations—overlap and contradiction.

I met Tsuka in the early 1970s, when Kato Ken'ichi and Miura Yoichi, two actors who were subsequently to become famous on their own, were acting in his group. (The list of famous actors who worked with Tsuka is long and illustrious.) They were doing plays at little out-of-the-way spaces like the Ikebukuro Theaterette. But I immediately recognized a playwright of immense talent.

Tsuka was, in those days, very much an "angry young man," just like playwrights in Britain in the 1950s and '60s. The title of John Osborne's 1956 play, *Look Back in Anger*, tells it all, and Tsuka was certainly one who was looking back at Japanese history and society with a good deal of anger.

It was not well known in those days that Tsuka was of Korean descent. He was a second-generation Korean Japanese whose real name was Kim Bon-un. His origins had a lot to do with his anger and his ironic take on Japanese society in such plays as *Murder Incident at Atami*, *Wait a Minute, Mr. Postman* and *For My Father Who Couldn't Die in the War*. In those days, however, people in the public eye did not advertise the fact that they were Korean. Tsuka's plays caused a boom in Japan, and by the late 1970s he was easily making the transition to bigger theaters like Van 99 Hall, where his *Story of a Stripper* was a big hit, starring another of his discoveries, actress Negishi Toshie.

But I must confess that I regret the fact that Tsuka did not become Japan's first "ethnic playwright." He could have exposed the deeply entrenched prejudices in the Japanese against Koreans. Why didn't he? For one thing, he wanted to be accepted as a Japanese playwright. I can well understand this. For another, Japanese society was still very unwelcoming to anyone who made a public fuss about things to do with ethnicity. The Japanese phrase *butsugi o kamosu* (to cause a stir) comes to mind. If you said you were Korean or you displayed pride in this, it was equivalent to causing a stir, particularly at a time when Japanese just wanted to pull together, consolidate gains and reach with one long arm into the markets of the world.

In this regard Japan has changed markedly, thanks to the opening up of society to minorities of all kinds in the late 1980s and '90s. But before then, it wasn't easy for anyone who was "too different" to make an issue out of that difference. If you kept your "problems" to yourself, you were respected and left alone. Japanese society didn't take to people being in your face. If you remained out of public sight, you could do pretty much what you wanted to in terms of lifestyle choices.

Tsuka, who dropped out of Keio University and forged his own directorial style, could have challenged and, perhaps, changed that culture of forced non-confrontationalism, taking the issue of Japanese-Korean relations into the open and informing the Japanese people of the suffering, both public and private, that Korean people have experienced at their hands. But though he was a rebel before his time, he chose to blend in rather than confront when it came to issues of minority ethnicity in Japan. Had he been writing now I am sure that he would have "come out." Many people of Korean origin living in Japan now use their Korean names, and there is much more open debate about issues affecting ethnic minorities who live in the country. Japanese signs at train stations now appear in Korean and Chinese as well as English.

The 1970s did open with a great deal of promise. There was the World's Fair in Osaka, Expo '70, which I visited five times, always at night (if you entered after 5 pm, the entrance fee was reduced by fifty percent). Looming over the site's entrance was Okamoto Taro's amazing "Tower of the Sun," a symbol of hope and promise if there ever was one. (It was at Expo '70 that I first met Andrzej Wajda, who had come there as head of a Polish film delegation. This friendship lasted until his death, at age ninety, in 2016. I was thrilled to be in Warsaw for the celebration of his eightieth birthday on March 6, 2006 and to spend the day with him and his wife, designer Krystyna Zachwatowicz, at their home.)

Expo '70 was a high point for the city. The 1970s witnessed the general decline in the importance of Osaka, economically, politically and culturally. Yokohama was overtaking Osaka as Japan's second city.

In general, the mood in Japan in the 1970s was one of cultural compromise. Director Ninagawa Yukio gave up doing plays in counterculture Shinjuku, opting for the big commercial stages of downtown Yurakucho. He received a phone call from producer Nakane Tadao at the commercial production house Toho, asking if he wanted to direct *Romeo and Juliet* at the cavernous Nissei Theater. Ninagawa took on the job and moved smoothly from alternative to commercial theater. To me—and I am not making any judgment here on whether this was a positive or a negative— this move symbolized the end of what was called the Little Theater Movement and the counterculture of Shinjuku.

I had become very enthusiastic about bringing my writer friends from Japan to Australia for them to experience not only the unique landscape of the country but also to see its theater and films. The 1970s were for Australia what the Taisho era (1912-1926) was for Japan: an opening up to the cultures of the world with a grand flourishing in the arts.

I was able to facilitate, through grants from the Australia-Japan Foundation, visits by poet Shiraishi Kazuko, with whom I had become good friends and whose work I greatly admired; and also of theater critic for the *Asahi Shinbun*, Senda Akihiko, who wrote in-depth articles about the Australian theater scene in his newspaper. Young Australians were flocking to Japan to absorb every aspect of Japanese culture. The influence in particular of Japanese ceramics, dance, fashion and graphic design on Australian culture deepened. Japanese people were beginning to discover Australia as well, though it was the environment—especially the koalas and kangaroos—that seemed to draw them there more than anything else. (The popularity on Japanese television of the frill-neck lizard in the 1980s fed this interest.)

But the thing that I wanted to do more than anything else was to invite my dear friend Inoue Hisashi and his family to Australia.

I had come to know him for the first time in 1974. We met at the Kioicho offices of the publisher Bungeishunju at noon on a clear and warm December's day. I had phoned to ask him if he would oblige me with an interview for the *Mainichi Daily News*, and he graciously accepted. Our first meal together was lunch that day at a little ramen restaurant near the publishing house.

It must be said that, at the time, while his work was becoming ever popular in Japan it was almost unknown to the outside world. For one thing, few foreign scholars or translators were interested in the contemporary theater, and for another, his novels were considered light, belonging in the category of "popular" and not the "pure" literature written by the "serious" writers that the primarily American scholars and translators saw as representing Japan. (It is a great relief that this ridiculous categorization of literature has broken down. I never accepted it from the very beginning, but, then again, I had been able to avoid the preferences of professors by not studying Japanese at an American university.)

Hisashi and I immediately clicked. We hadn't been talking ten minutes when I said that Miyazawa Kenji was the greatest Japanese writer of the twentieth century and he agreed, saying, "Kenji will be the only twentieth-century Japanese author whose name will live on in later centuries." We shook hands, smiling at each other, and that handshake forged a bond of friendship that grew and grew over the years. (Please recall how rare these opinions were at the time. Kenji was then considered a minor author of children's literature by the literary establishment.)

"But there is one more such writer in Japan," I said. "You."

I wasn't flattering him. I had seen most of his plays up to that time, as well as read several novels. To me, his sense of humor was a weapon to attack hypocrisy and senseless violence. I knew then in my bones that he was going to be a powerful voice on the Japanese stage and literary scene.

On subsequent visits to Japan from Australia in the 1970s, I stayed at his home in Ichikawa and there encountered many wonderful people. I met Tani Kei, who amused us with a story of how he avoided getting mugged on a New York street by jumping up, thrusting his open hands forward and pretending to be a karate champion. (He took his stage name from Danny Kaye.) The great journalist, activist and feminist Matsui Yayori stands out vividly in my memory. I praised her for writing about women's issues, particularly in an Asian context, in the *Asahi Shinbun*.

"But, Pulvers-san," she said, "the *Asahi* is as awful on this as the other media, maybe even worse than what you see in Japanese society in general."

It was true of newspapers in all countries at the time. The world of journalism was seen as a hard-nosed closed-fisted man's world. That there are now many senior female journalists in Japan is a sign of great progress in this country, and Matsui Yayori was one of the pioneers in that progress.

After returning to Australia, in January 1978 from my long stay at the Inoue home and the trip to Yaeyama, my life started to change in ways that I myself was unaware of. I had met Susan and fallen in love. But I was still married and wracked with pangs of conscience over my own selfish actions. This created a situation in which three people were miserable. I was being cruel to two women, both of whom I felt affection for. When this happens to anyone, man or woman, the only solution is for a swift, if painful, decision of choice.

While there were problems like these in my personal life, my career had begun to flourish for the first time. My plays were being produced at bigger theaters in Australia and actually getting positive reviews. I was writing and narrating radio shows almost weekly and generating articles for a host of publications. *Shingeki* magazine had published two more plays, *Yamashita* and *General MacArthur in Australia*. And, although I thoroughly enjoyed teaching at the ANU, I felt that it was time to become a fulltime writer and director.

At the very end of the 1979 I quit my university job to become Playwright-in-Residence at the Playbox Theatre in Melbourne. I was to direct many plays there, some of my own and some by other playwrights, and was to write frequently for *The Age*, Melbourne's leading daily newspaper, and continue to write and narrate radio shows for ABC. My income may have dropped by two-thirds when I left academia, but I felt for the first time in my life that I was living off my talents. I felt rich, because I was doing what I wanted to do.

On my first day in Melbourne I walked into a coffee shop, ordered an espresso, plonked the sixty cents that it cost on the counter, drank the espresso down and blurted out, "I'm free!" A bearded guy wearing a bead necklace next to me leaned against the counter, smirked and said, "Well good for you, mate!"

I guess the move from Canberra to Melbourne, from a safe and well-paying job at a university to an unpredictable and low-paying job at a theater, was one that I had made of my own volition. Or was it? Perhaps my nature that craves something new and unknown, as if insecurity was the mother of change, had created for me another unimaginable and miraculous moment.

All I could do was picture myself as a little red dragonfly perched on the end of a long pole, waiting for the next moment in time.

7

A DIALOGUE WITH THE JAPANESE PEOPLE

There is a beautiful cherry blossom tree just beside the Sakurakan public bathhouse in Ikegami, a five-minute walk from the last home I inhabited in Tokyo. A branch of this cherry blossom tree hangs high over the roof, and just below the branch is an opening in the roof. The petals from the branch flutter down into the *rotenburo* below. Rotenburo is the word for an "outdoor bath," but it is used loosely in Japan. Some of the rotenburo are exposed to the outside air only through a window or an opening in the roof. The ones in the countryside, however, are generally truly outdoors, giving an extra meaning to the word "public" in "public bath."

The day after Inoue Hisashi died on April 9, 2010, a Friday, I went, as I did every week, to Sakurakan, whose baths are filled with dark charcoal-colored water that is pumped up from deep below the ground. There are not many of these pure black water public bathhouses in Japan. This one, at Ikegami, is certified by the government as genuine. The black water is said to have medicinal properties more effective than those in your ordinary clear-water baths.

That Friday, in the evening, a handful of cherry blossom petals came floating down onto the smoky surface of the water. Tears welled in my eyes ... and, from then on I associated the falling of the cherry blossoms solely with the passing of my dear and wonderful friend, Inoue Hisashi.

Over the hundreds of hours we spent together during a friendship that lasted thirty-five years, we talked about absolutely everything, from onomatopoeia in the works of Miyazawa-zawa Kenji to Article 9 of the Japanese Constitution that forever denounces armed belligerency; from the taste of the delicious *kinpira gobo*, or spicy burdock, that his Fukushima mother-in-law made to the films of the Marx Brothers. I wanted very much for the rest of the world to know about the mind and talent of this superlative writer, and, with his permission, started translating his work, beginning with his novel *The Fortunes of Father Mockinpott*.

And then an idea struck me. I would invite Hisashi, his wife Yoshiko and their three daughters, Miyako, Aya and Maya to Canberra for a year. I felt that Hisashi, who had never lived overseas, would enjoy being away from Japan for a while. He had become quite popular as a writer and commentator on society and was writing as many as two thousand Japanese pages every month— and this was by hand! (That's roughly the equivalent of twenty or thirty pages of an English-language book per day.) Perhaps being away from Japan would give him some time to relax and think.

I was staying at the Inoue home in Ichikawa, a town in Chiba prefecture just over the Tokyo-Chiba border, on New Year's Eve, 1975. Another guest was Ozawa Shoichi. That night a team from NHK had also come to Ichikawa to record a message for the new year for "Yuku Toshi Kuru Toshi," a popular spot on national television broadcast before midnight on New Year's Eve. The moment the live broadcast began, Ozawa blurted out, "Inoue is going to Austria next year … wait, I mean Australia!" It was even an old joke in those days, but it still got a laugh in Japan.

I will never forget the late summer's day that the Inoues arrived in Canberra. It was early March and exceedingly hot and dry. Canberra today has a population of nearly 400,000, but at that time it was less than half that. The airport, now a huge modern building, was then the size of a large bungalow, with amenities befitting that variety of building. I can picture the five Inoues sitting while waiting for their luggage to appear. What adventures, I wondered, were ahead of them?

I had made a big mistake in the planning of their stay in renting a flat for them across the street from the one in which I lived. I had thought that this convenience would allow me to come to their assistance quickly whenever they might need me. But the flat, with only two bedrooms, was far too small for them. Besides,

Hisashi used to write all through the night and needed a separate room for himself as a study. Another thing that was too small was their mailbox in the block of flats. He would receive an enormous amount of mail from Japan, always special delivery and often registered. Neither the little opening in the metal nor the mailbox itself could cope with the deliveries. And yet, being Japanese and guests, the Inoues never complained to me in any way about their accommodation.

Hisashi also had many visitors in Canberra, one of them Shiba Ryotaro, the famous writer of historical novels, who was on his way to Thursday Island to do research for a book on the Japanese pearl divers and the Japanese-run brothels there before the war. I asked Shiba Ryotaro where he lived in Japan.

"In East Osaka."

"East Osaka? Isn't that a rough area where some thieves live?"

"Yes, they do live there. But they all go out at night to do their work so it's okay."

The three Inoue girls attended the nearby Turner Primary School. I think they enjoyed themselves, despite the language barrier. I recall them telling me that the thing that most surprised them was that you could get ice cream in the school shop. Yoshiko did her best to cope with the enormous change in lifestyle, although I know she felt isolated from her usual milieu of editors, publishers and journalists in Tokyo. Back in Ichikawa, she was her husband's manager, and she kept editors, publishers and journalists waiting and entertained while he, never one to be on time for a deadline, was in his cramped little study writing page after page in his very careful hand.

A word about Hisashi's writing and his view on deadlines.

If you ever see his manuscripts you will notice that each character or letter is placed clearly and legibly within the lines of each box on the paper. It isn't so much as if he is writing as planting words, performing a kind of literary rice-planting ritual, seedling by seedling. As for deadlines, he often got things done just by the skin of his teeth, and once was so late that a leading literary monthly had to publish blank pages. Some newspapers had cars and drivers waiting outside the house for hours on end with their motors running, something that is against the law in many countries today. In those days turning off your engine was seen as a sign of slack. No one worried then about the pollution of exhaust fumes from idling the car. The editors wanted to show how eager they were by being ready to leave the instant they had their copy in hand.

"When is the final deadline?" I once asked him about a particular story.

The Japanese word for "deadline" is *shimekiri*. He burst into a laugh.

"What? The final shimekiri? What do you mean?"

"Well, if you can't keep your deadline, isn't there another deadline after it that's really a deadline?"

"No," he chuckled. "A shimekiri is a shimekiri. It is the last. There's no shimekiri after it."

I think that Inoue Hisashi, founder of the "Mental Block Book Depository" that he established in his home prefecture of Yamagata, would have been happier had he been a writer in a country that had movable deadlines.

On the very first day in Canberra I walked with him from his flat into town, a walk of about twenty minutes. I brought up something that was very awkward to talk about. I cannot forget that conversation and how it came back to haunt me in 2010.

"You know the reason why I asked you to come to Canberra, besides, of course, to advise our students of Japanese at the university?" I asked.

He looked puzzled, shaking his head.

"Because I wanted you to give up smoking."

"Ah," he said.

Hisashi was a heavy smoker, as were most writers at the time. He was smoking about sixty cigarettes a day then, on some days a hundred, puffing away in a tiny closed-off closet-like room where the smoke circulated back into his lungs. In fact he did give up cigarettes in Canberra, but only for ten days. When, in the autumn of 2009, I learned that he had been diagnosed with lung cancer, that walk into town, under a clear and sunny Canberra sky, came back to me. My playwright friend Tsuka Kohei also died of lung cancer, some three months after Hisashi. I just wish that I had had the power over Hisashi to stop him from smoking way back in 1976.

A few days after the Inoues arrived in Canberra we all flew to Adelaide, where Hisashi gave a wonderful talk on the Japanese sense of humor for Writers' Week at the Adelaide Festival of the Arts.

Now, it must be said that Hisashi and Yoshiko hated flying. Once they drove me to Narita Airport to see me off and we sat in the restaurant waiting for my flight. Every time a plane took off he looked through the big window onto the runway, cocked his head and said, "Unbelievable." The flight from Canberra to Adelaide was fairly smooth, but at one point the plane dropped suddenly, causing Yoshiko to shriek and throw the cards (she was playing with one of her daughters) high into the air.

Yoshiko ended up staying in Canberra for only three months, leaving Hisashi and their eldest daughter, Miyako, in Canberra. Hisashi and Miyako followed two months later. I was sad that they all hadn't stayed for the planned year. But in a sense the plan was not realistic from the start. Hisashi was entering the prime of his career. Staying away from Japan for a year, and in a faraway and isolated place such as Canberra, was really not an option.

While in Canberra Hisashi wrote one of his best plays, *Rain*, and also did research for his novel about Japanese POWs in Australia during the war, *The Yellow Rats*. But I think he gained something very important by getting away from Japan for half a year and experiencing a place as different from Tokyo as Canberra. This is what he said to me in the early 1980s ...

> The biggest experience that I got out of going to Australia was the realization that I'm a foreigner too. I lost the feeling of trepidation and strangeness regarding how we Japanese look at

the outside world. And thanks to living in Australia, it dawned on me that we're all just humans who happen to be born on this little planet, just fellow humans who are doing our best to survive the era we are in together. That's the most important thing I gained, and I have my going to Australia to thank for it.

Hisashi was, above all, a humanist. Where did his inspiration come from?

"I will never get out of my mind," he told me back in the mid-1970s, "the suffering of the people of Tohoku who streamed into Tokyo for many decades before and after the war looking for work, uprooted and having to scrounge around for sustenance."

The primary theme running through his writing is the plight of the weak and their struggle to keep their head above water in a heartless society. He never let his gaze slip from society's dispossessed. He strove to give the underdog the benefit of the doubt and the tools to rectify their helpless circumstances.

I am writing this book to remind people about the Japanese qualities of compassion, consideration and warm tenderness that they have shown to others. So much of the narrative of Japan embraced in some parts of Asia, Europe and the United States has been dominated first by the atrocities committed during the fifteen years of war in Asia and the Pacific (1931-45) and subsequently by the image of the Japanese as dark-suited "samurai salarymen" marching in step to the company's tune.

In the everyday struggles of life it is easy to forget that many other people are less fortunate than you. We need our Miyazawa Kenjis and Inoue Hisashis to remind us that our personal happiness depends upon the happiness of the countless people we do not know and will never know, people living not only in other parts of Japan but in all countries around the world. We must look to culture for the inspiration on how to reach out to them.

"I want to show people who have little power the way to use their ingenuity in order to make their presence felt, so that they may gain some advantage in their misery," Hisashi said to me.

It is precisely these humanistic themes that run through his more than sixty plays and forty novels. In addition to these, he published some fifty books of essays and miscellany, virtually all of them permeated by a scholarly approach to subject.

In the early 1980s, while working as literary editor at the *Mainichi Daily News*, I decided to translate and serialize his historical novel on the life of Luis Frois, the Portuguese missionary of the sixteenth century, *My Friend Frois*. This novel includes many references in the text to the names of ancient ships and the like, all of which were in katakana, the alphabet used primarily for foreign words. It was long before the era of the internet when these things could be readily looked up.

"I'm having trouble with the historical references," I said to him on the phone. "Could you send me a few of the books or whatever you used for research?"

"Sure. I'll get them out to you by courier."

Two days later a huge box of books was delivered to my home. Every volume had scores of highlighted lines. I phoned him again.

"I received the books, and thank you so much. But, my God, did you really do such prodigious research for the Frois novel?"

"Well," he said, "I sent you only about one-third of what I used. Want the rest, too?"

"No, no. It's enough. Thank you!"

Hisashi, who loved books, established the book depository in his old hometown, eventually sending them a whopping 200,000 volumes from his personal library. One of the reasons he was notorious for keeping directors, actors, publishers and editors waiting for his scripts and manuscripts was due to the fact that he delved deeply into minute historical detail for every one of his works, making it impossible to deliver on time. He spent most of his time at home in his study poring over books, often not going out of the house for days on end. He was essentially a shy and very reserved man. He didn't like partying. He had disdain for Japanese men who easily became inebriated and lost their inhibitions. (This disdain stemmed, in part, from his aversion to the behavior of his stepfather, a man, by his account, who became crude and violent when drunk.)

Despite the scrupulous attention to detail—especially in the kind of language a particular character in a particular era or setting would use—Hisashi never lost sight of the big picture. And the big picture for him was his dialogue with the Japanese people over their history, culture and future.

In his plays he took up the lives of famous Japanese people, from writers as disparate in temperament and style as Matsuo Basho, Higuchi Ichiyo, Natsume Soseki, Miyazawa Kenji and Dazai Osamu to generals (Nogi Maresuke) and monks (Dogen). These are warts-and-all portraits. Hisashi was intrigued not by those elements in their personalities and character that set them apart from ordinary people, but rather those that bound them to the commonplace. These characters, with their quirks and foibles, have resonated with audiences, forming a human-based—as opposed to a conceptual, sociological or ideological—notion of what it means to be Japanese in our day and age.

This character-centered humanist approach set him apart from most of his playwright contemporaries, such as Terayama Shuji and Kara Juro. The moment I saw his play *The Adventures of Dogen* in 1971, I was attracted to his ingenious use of language, his cutting humor and his radically critical take on the orthodoxies and contraints of Japanese culture. And yet Hisashi's name was somehow being left out of critical discussions about the revolution that Japanese theater had undergone in the 1960s and '70s. Because his dramaturgy was ostensibly less radical than that of the two playwrights mentioned above and because he was, thanks in large part to the soft humor in his works, reaching wide audiences, he was not easy to categorize as an "underground" playwright.

"You are an amazing humorist," I said to him when I first met him in 1974.

"Thank you. But that's not such a good thing in Japan. Japanese critics prefer serious writers. They look down on humor."

The critics and scholars long failed to see that lurking behind

Inoue Hisashi's intricate wordplay and the clever situation-comedy-like skits and encounters within his plays and novels was a slyly concealed and sharply honed blade aimed straight at the heart of authority. Ironically, now that he is gone, many people looking over his entire body of work have begun to see just how deftly he wielded his sword of satire. Humor for him was satire; satire, a weapon in the hands of the weak.

Even the villains in his plays are treated with the psychological respect he feels they, as fully-drawn characters, deserve. One of his favorite novels was Charles Dickens's *David Copperfield*; and his works shared with those of Dickens the astute inner depiction of evil, not only in its effects but also in its causes.

Now that we can look back at his entire massive body of work, I think we can see a pattern emerging, a pattern that both preceded and reflected the very transformation of Japan since the 1990s into a country ready to confront its social problems head on.

Hisashi started out his writing career as a literary entertainer. In the town where he was born, Komatsumachi, there was a little theater called Komatsuza, which he took as the name of his own theater company when he established it in 1984. Every night "famous" entertainers would appear in this small Yamagata town. Of course, these were impersonators. But they were so comically convincing, it hardly mattered. Seeing these performers, and later working at the France Theater, a raunchy vaudeville venue in Asakusa, provided Hisashi as a child and young man with his first burst of inspiration to become a writer.

He co-wrote a television puppet drama series that became immensely popular with children and adults alike, *Hyokkori Hyotanjima* (which might be called "Pop-up Island off its Gourd"), that ran on NHK television from 1964 to 1969. From there he penned his first professionally produced play, *The Japanese Navel*. His aim then was solely to entertain. But in 1973 when his masterpiece *The Blind Master Yabuhara* was produced, I believe Hisashi began to see himself as a socially committed playwright. And the two themes—light entertainment, with music, wordplay and humor on the one hand, and a deadly serious social message on the other—continued to combine in his plays and novels for the rest of his life.

This genre of comic satire is evident in the ancient culture of kyogen, in many bunraku (traditional puppet) plays and in the arts of the traveling performers so highly valued by Ozawa Shoichi (he compiled a huge audio library of them). It also pervades the modern culture, in novels by Soseki such as *Botchan* and *I am a Cat*, the short stories of Akutagawa Ryunosuke and particularly his novella *Kappa*, the black humor of Sakaguchi Ango in works like *In the Woods Beneath the Cherry Blossoms in Full Bloom*, the literature of contemporary science fiction author Tsutsui Yasutaka such as *Salmonella Man on Planet Porno*, and just about all the plays of Betsuyaku Minoru, to mention only a very small part of this fantastic modern Japanese tradition. Around the world it is a lesser known feature of Japanese culture, but it is nonetheless as mainstream as the more austere and minimalistic arts.

Needless to say, writers do not just make sudden and arbitrary transformations. In 1964 NHK produced Hisashi's radio play about a small region in Tohoku called Kirikiri that declares independence from Japan, *Kirikiri Goes Independent*. Seventeen years later, in 1981, he published this as a novel that quickly became a bestseller. He had long kept in his heart this revolutionary idea of a region of Japan, in his native Tohoku of course, breaking away from the nation. This novel is an attack on the centralized culture of Tokyo imposed on people around the country. It is Hisashi's bittersweet revenge struck in the name of all of those poverty-stricken people compelled to leave their home in search of a decent living in the nation's capital.

I am writing quite a lot about the work of Inoue Hisashi in this book, but there is a reason. I want to show you that he had the spirit of rebellion in his gut, that he loved and respected the reader and the audience more than anything and saw his role as making them laugh, cry and learn. This is the very kind of Japanese culture that can reach out to the world.

A DIALOGUE WITH THE JAPANESE PEOPLE

I have a tape of an hour-long interview that Hisashi did for NHK radio in August 1992. He talks in that interview about the war and about one of his favorite topics, the cultivation of rice and its place in Japanese culture, but he does not mention Hiroshima or Nagasaki. In fact Hisashi was not, for many years, particularly interested in the culture of western Japan or points south of that.

But something changed in him, I believe. Perhaps it was the popping of the economic bubble that caused him to re-evaluate Japan's role in the world. I don't know. But in the early 1990s he began to turn his vision in the direction of Hiroshima and Nagasaki and see the need to make the tragedy of those two cities universal, that is, understood and felt not only by people in Japan but by people all over the world. With his play *Chichi to Kuraseba*, which I translated into English under the title *The Face of Jizo*, Hisashi turned all of us into victims of the atom bombs.

Then in 2003 he wrote a play for recitation titled *Mizu no Tegami*. (I translated this play for presentation at the 2010 International PEN Congress in Tokyo under the title *The Water Letters*.) This is a powerful work about how we are linked all over the world by water. To me this theme took on an even more poignant significance following the triple tragedy that initially struck Tohoku on March 11, 2011 in the form of an earthquake of magnitude nine, a tsunami that in places reached heights of more than 130 feet, and radioactive fallout that spread in the region and beyond. That tragedy, with its as yet unresolved aftermath, occurred not only in Tohoku but in every country on the planet.

In the year before he died Hisashi was working on a play set in Okinawa. He said to me, "We Japanese must come to terms with what happened in Okinawa during the war and what Okinawa represents for us today."

I saw him for the last time on October 3, 2009, at the opening of his play about the life and murder in custody of the proletarian author Kobayashi Takiji, *Suite Slaughter*.

"You look good," I said.

But he didn't.

"Really? Actually, I'm falling apart at the seams. I'd be lucky to have another ten years in me."

As it turned out, a couple of weeks after that he was diagnosed with the lung cancer that killed him less than six months later.

There is an expression in Japanese about just such a person as Inoue Hisashi. It is *yojin o motte kaegatai*. In English we might say, "There will never be another one like him."

The voice for reason, peace and hope that he symbolized project—if I may use a word from the stage—far and wide in Japan. If that voice manages to cross over the oceans and to be heard by people in other countries, then my dear, dear gentle friend Inoue Hisashi will come to represent the generous, open-minded, kindhearted and peaceful face of this country.

What more could be asked of any writer? It is precisely these qualities that I would ask each and every Japanese person to possess and show to the world in the years to come.

8

LIKE THE FISH WHO LIVE IN THE DEPTHS OF THE SEA

In June 1982 Susan and I set out on what was to be a remarkable journey.

We flew from Melbourne to Tokyo and went straight from Narita Airport to the Inoue home in Ichikawa. Hisashi had never met Susan before and I was anxious to introduce her. (A few years later, he, too, was to separate from his wife Yoshiko and remarry.) There was to be a costume coordination and fitting for Oshima Nagisa's upcoming film *Merry Christmas, Mr. Lawrence* in the beginning of July, and I was eager, in the interim, to take Susan up to my favorite part of Japan, Tohoku.

The Tohoku shinkansen between Omiya and Morioka had opened on June 23 of that year, and a couple of days later we were on it on our way to our first stop, Hanamaki. Susan had come to love Kenji's stories and poems, too. Though we were not yet married (I was still waiting for my divorce to come through), this trip was a kind of honeymoon.

I took her to all of the places in Hanamaki associated with Kenji, including the English Coast, the Las Chijin Kyokai building where Kenji had, for a short time, lived and taught, and Hanamaki Onsen. We stayed up at Dai Onsen, which Kenji had also visited, bathed in and written a short story about. We walked all around Koiwai Farm that figures so significantly in his writing. We must have been the only foreigners who spent their honeymoon at Koiwai Farm surrounded by a lot of cows. I cherish the photo I have of Susan and me by a fence under a beautiful Iwate sky.

We went to Miyako, that lovely port so tragically struck by the tsunami in 2011, and took a boat up the Rikuchu Coast. The weather was warm, but cooled by the sea breeze; and I thought, already age thirty-eight, that a new life was ahead of me. I was truly, deeply, passionately in love for the first time in my life, and we both wanted children. We didn't know then that Susan was pregnant with our first child.

We returned to Tokyo to team up with the staff and actors of *Merry Christmas, Mr. Lawrence*, which everyone was referring to as *Senmeri*, its abbreviated Japanese title. What is called in Japanese the "crank in" (a term borrowed from the old days in Hollywood when a camera was actually cranked) was to begin in a few weeks' time. Oshima Nagisa and I had become very close friends by then. He was kind enough to give Susan a job on the film too, so that we could be together. She had had nursing experience in Melbourne, and so she became the staff nurse for *Senmeri* and appears as such in the credits under her maiden name, Susan Nicholas. She also tied all of the bandages for the POWs in the film, so she had an artistic input as well.

I had enormous respect for Oshima Nagisa as a filmmaker and today consider him on a par with Ozu Yasujiro and Kurosawa Akira. I subsequently became friends with film directors Yamada Yoji and Shinoda Masahiro, even appearing in one of Shinoda's films, *Spy Sorge*. But I felt the closest affinities with Oshima, a man who gave a voice to an entire generation of young people in Japan.

Oshima had come to Australia in August 1981 at the invitation of the National Film Theatre of Australia for a lecture tour on the occasion of a retrospective of his films. I was his guide and interpreter. As we traveled from Melbourne to Sydney and Canberra, we realized that we shared a view of what constitutes real drama. What he told me a couple of years later goes a long way in clarifying the human drama he depicts on film.

"What I like to do essentially is drive people into the midst of an extreme situation," he said, "then observe their responses."

The clue to understanding the themes in his films is "extreme situation." In his film *Taiyo no Hakaba* (*The Sun's Burial*), made in 1960, he examines life in the dosshouse district of Osaka and the rules of teenage survival that applied there. Here it was the shining era of Japanese economic growth, and a film director was turning our attention to bleak industrial Japan and the extreme alienation it engendered, particularly in the young. How prophetic is that! (Some of the themes taken up years later by Murakami Haruki, particularly the aimlessness and isolation of the individual, are similar to those in the Oshima films of the 1960s.)

It just so happened that two of my plays were on in Melbourne when he was there for the retrospective, and I took him to see them. This was, I later learned, decisive in his choosing me to be assistant director on *Senmeri*. There were already quite a few foreigners who spoke Japanese well enough to do the job. But Oshima wanted someone who knew how to talk to actors—that is, diplomatically, gently, constructively. If the wrong tone was taken in interpreting the director's wishes, the actors might become upset and lose the moment.

When we were on the plane traveling from Melbourne to Sydney he handed me a film script written in English. It was an early draft of *Senmeri*. I read it, finishing it just before we landed.

"What do you think?" he asked.

"It's amazing. Are you going to make this?"

He paused for a long moment, staring me in the eye.

"Maybe."

I didn't hear from him for over seven months after his return to Japan until, one day in April 1982, a letter arrived. It was just one page long, written, of course, in Japanese. He wrote that he had found the money to make *Senmeri*, which he was shooting in the summer, and would I be his assistant.

Now, when we read a letter with either very good or very bad news, we may not be able to take it in at first. A kind of mental block may be protecting us from shock. I stared at the page for a few minutes, thinking, "Is this really what he is asking me to do? Maybe I am not understanding the Japanese properly and he is simply asking me to recommend someone to be his assistant." Finally, after about five minutes of staring at the page, it dawned on me that I could be his assistant. When Susan came back from nursing at the hospital I told her the news.

"Darling, Oshima wants me to be his assistant director. And after the filming is over, I want to go back home to Japan to live. I am really happier there than here."

"So am I. Let's go," she said.

With tears in my eyes I hugged her very tight. We were to start on a fantastic adventure again, one that led us to have four children who were born, raised and educated in Japan.

And so, in the summer of 1982, a large cast from Japan, Britain, Australia and New Zealand—led by David Bowie, comedian and later film director "Beat" Takeshi (Kitano Takeshi), actor Tom Conti and musician Sakamoto Ryuichi—assembled on the unspoiled and, in many ways, idyllic island of Rarotonga in the Cook Islands, some three hours by air northeast of Auckland, New Zealand, to re-enact the arbitrary brutalities and unforeseeable intimacies of the Japanese prisoner-of-war camp. The actual war had passed Rarotonga right by. One old resident told me that during the entire war he saw only a single warship on the horizon.

My day began at 4:45 in the morning racing through a grove of tall coconut palms to the director's car. The reason this was necessary was that it wouldn't do for me, the driver, to turn the ignition key later on, with director Oshima Nagisa and cinematographer Narushima Toichiro in the back seat, only to find that the engine of the rusting Toyota wouldn't start up. The reason for my racing through the grove was to dodge the coconuts that were sailing downward, like so many bombs, in the gale-like winds of the island.

No sight on the shoot was as heartwarming as that seen every day at breakfast. The production had taken up nearly every room of the main hotel on the island and each morning the dining room was invaded, if you will, by a horde of actors in the uniforms of their roles: Japanese soldiers, with their flap-back jungle hats, rifles resting against their tables; and POW Westerners, plucked from among the skinniest and most emaciated young men we could find on the streets of Auckland, outfitted in tatters.

There they sat together around their tables—merciless soldiers and pitiful prisoners—digging into mounds of runny eggs smothered in thick fatty streaks of bacon, stacks of English muffins and mountains of luscious papaya, refilling each other's coffee cups, gabbing away in a comical mishmash of Japanese and English and occasionally breaking into raucous laughter, until meeting on the set and slipping comfortably into the roles of sadistic torturer and brutalized victim.

One morning, feeling their oats, and in a gesture of playful camaraderie, a few of the Japanese and New Zealand extras hoisted the flag of the Imperial Japanese Navy up the flagpole on the hotel roof. This must have shocked the living daylights out of a small group of elderly New Zealand tourists arriving in their minivan from the airport. I saw them enter the dining room for their first breakfast on the island. They froze in their tracks at the sight of armed Japanese soldiers mingling with Western prisoners in scarecrow rags. The memory of soldiers Yokoi Shoichi and Onoda Hiroo emerging from their jungle hideouts in 1972 and 1974 was still fresh in people's minds. Could it be that hostilities were still in progress on this remote island in the middle of the Pacific?

The making of *Senmeri* symbolizes a postwar watershed in Japanese culture. The amicability displayed off the set by the Japanese and nonJapanese actors marked, to my mind, an opening up on both sides, a tacit recognition that the war in the Pacific, which had ended thirty-seven years earlier, was not their war and that they were not going to allow it to define their personal relationships.

Young people in any country are not responsible for the crimes committed by their parents, grandparents or ancestors. They are only responsible for not permitting those crimes to be committed again. The best way to ensure that this sense of responsibility takes hold in them is for them to have a thorough knowledge of their country's past and for them to redress the evils of that past by offering unmitigated goodwill, openhearted friendship and, when necessary, generous aid to people in countries who have suffered the ills of intolerance, colonialism and poverty at the hands of their forebears. The young Japanese and nonJapanese who worked together on *Senmeri*, a film about reconciliation in war, with such friendly enthusiasm represent a symbol of that generosity and goodwill.

Working on the beautiful tropical island of Rarotonga and watching at close hand how Oshima Nagisa made his films was the experience of a lifetime. It was also inspiring to see how production designer Toda Jusho, whose brilliant work on Kobayashi Masaki's *Kwaidan* and *Seppuku* (*Harakiri*) I consider world-class masterpieces of film design, created the sets on an island with a limited amount of resources, basically just heaps of wood and palm fronds. The entire experience became for me the training ground for my own work on *Star Sand* thirty-four years later.

Oshima Nagisa as a man and artist had those qualities that I deeply admire in the Japanese: rebelliousness combined with a profound love of his culture; iconoclasm in the re-creation in art of "extreme situations" infused with an optimistic and genuinely polite nature. The young people of Japan need to learn about the conflicts and resolutions in their recent history by going back again and again to the films of Oshima Nagisa.

After the "crank up" Susan and I returned to Melbourne from Rarotonga and Auckland (the two locations for *Senmeri*), packed our personal effects, stopped off in Canberra to visit Susan's parents, who were delighted that their first grandchild was going to be born early the next year, 1983, and flew to Narita Airport, where Inoue Yoshiko was kind enough to meet us and take us to Ichikawa. Without the kindness and generosity of the Inoues, I doubt that I would have ever felt so much at home in Tokyo. After all, I had never really lived in Tokyo, only stayed there for some months at a time. My home in Japan was Kyoto, specifically a spot by the Deep Muddy Pond.

I took up the job at the *Mainichi Daily News*, creating a Monday page of articles and features on culture called Monday Arts, and

Susan and I started looking for a place to live. We eventually found a little attached house near Tsurigane Pond in Soshigaya 5-chome, about ten minutes' walk down the shopping street from Soshigaya Okura Station on the Odakyu Line. As it turned out Sakamoto Ryuichi, with whom I had worked on *Senmeri* and become good friends, had grown up not far from there. Ryuichi had attended Soshigaya Primary School. Another good friend, actor Midori Mako, who I had seen on stage in stunningly theatrical plays by her troupe Dainana Byoto (Ward Seven), lived not far away in Soshigaya 3-chome. Mako and her partner, brilliant actor Ishibashi Renji, visited us at home; and I cherish photos of them holding our children. (Again this all became linked, decades later, to *Star Sand*. I filmed the last scene of the film between Midori Mako and young star Yoshioka Riho at Tsurigane Pond, a stone's throw from where Susan and I had lived so long before.)

Monday Arts brought together a group of Japanese writers, poets, playwrights, actors, translators and other artists who had never appeared before on the pages of Japan's English-language dailies. These included Murakami Haruki (not yet the world-famous author he became), Inoue Hisashi, author Muramatsu Tomomi, poet Tomioka Taeko, author Shiina Makoto, poet Shiraishi Kazuko, playwright Kara Juro, translator and scholar Takahashi Yasunari, fashion designer Yamamoto Kansai, architect Isozaki Arata, translator Odashima Yuji, playwright Noda Hideki, playwright Betsuyaku Minoru, author Tsutsui Yasutaka, poet Tanikawa Shuntaro, poet Tamura Ryuichi, and many others. I contacted them and they wrote articles in Japanese that I translated for Monday Arts. The English-language dailies had, up till then, not been strong on introducing contemporary Japanese culture to their readers. They had, after all, started life as information sheets for the foreign community, concentrating primarily on commerce and diplomacy and later hometown sports game scores. I wanted that to change.

I was thrilled to get the writer I thought most deserving of the Nobel Prize in Literature, Ibuse Masuji, on my page, too.

Ibuse's subtle sense of self-deprecating humor and his humanistic approach to characters, especially in his novel about Hiroshima that I consider a world classic, *Black Rain*, made him the kind of Japanese writer I wanted the world to take notice of. Oshima Nagisa wrote a regular Monday Arts film criticism column as well.

Our son, Jeremy, was born on February 28, 1983 at the National Okura Hospital, where our first daughter, Alice, and our second daughter, Sophie, were also born. Our last child, Lucy, was born at the Kyoto Prefectural Hospital, becoming our only "Kansai (western Japan) child." I went every day to the hospital to visit Susan when she was at the Okura Hospital, and was grateful that across the street there was an excellent sushi restaurant and a public bathhouse. While poor Susan was waiting for our son, and later our two daughters, to be born and recovering from the births, I was enjoying the luxury of bath and sushi. Childbirth is a very unfair bargain indeed. The man's job is done in thirty seconds—well, maybe a tad longer—and the woman has all the excruciating pain, but also all of the joys of motherhood.

One thing that can be said for the 1980s in Japan is that the decade was exceedingly exciting. In Japan it was called "the feeling era." The country was prospering while the U.S. was bogged down in slow growth and a disastrous savings-and-loan scandal. Maybe Herman Kahn was right and Japan would be number one. The price of land in Tokyo and other big cities was skyrocketing. Almost no one suspected at the time that we were living on the skin of a huge bubble.

My career started to take off in the 1980s. I was writing fulltime not only for my paper, the *Mainichi Daily News*, but also regularly for Japanese-language newspapers and magazines. And I started to appear on television, particularly after the success of a two-part TBS show, *Subarashiki Nakama* (*Wonderful Friends*). The foreigner boom on TV was about to take place, and these two episodes of *Wonderful Friends* that I emceed were the first ones featuring all foreigners, including singer Agnes Chan from Hong Kong, body-builder Chuck Wilson from the U.S. and the Italian

LIKE THE FISH WHO LIVE IN THE DEPTHS   125

singer Rosanna. In subsequent years appearances on many talk shows followed, both serious and not so serious. These included variety shows starring popular TV personalities Yamada Kuniko and Shimada Shinsuke, as well as talk shows on politics and social issues such as *Sunday Project* and *Asa made no Nama Terebi* (*Live TV till Morning*). The latter was filmed live from midnight to morning when, it turned out, many of the taboos observed by the media in Japan were free to be discussed. I also appeared together as a regular with author and journalist Hayashi Mariko on the interview NHK show *Studio L*.

They were heady times. The culture of the 1980s was a culture dominated by youth. The young people of Japan had money in their pocket for the first time—maybe not money to burn but surely enough to go around. And they spent it on those things that all people desired: food, fashion, entertainment, cars, travel and new technology (computers and video games had just begun to take Japan and the world by storm). By no means was it only young people seeking all this out. There was an unprecedented gourmet boom in Japan. New restaurants and fashion outlets were springing up all over the country, particularly in Tokyo. The three buzzwords of the decade were *kokusaika* (internationalization), *torendi* (trendy) and *now-i* (totally now). It was a time of blind optimism, when "experts" on talk shows boasted that Japan was the greatest country to live in in the world, a country without crime, drugs, child abuse, sexual harassment (which as a word didn't come into popular usage in the language until the late 1980s; people still called it *seiteki-iyagarase*, a literal translation of the English) or presumably any other social evil.

I was beginning to get worried. The fishmonger in the Soshigaya shopping street wore a Louis Vuitton apron (no doubt fake). I knew that horrible social problems existed in Japan as they did elsewhere, though I always loved living and bringing up children here because it was so safe for them outside the house. Where else in a major industrialized city of the world could your little children travel on buses and trains by themselves? This is surely one of the greatest aspects of Japanese freedom, and the rest of the world should envy Japan for it: the freedom to feel and be safe on the streets day or night.

I was not worried about the young people and their sense of fun that by its very nature debunked the previous generation's overseriousness. This kind of rebellion was encouraging; and I saw in a young playwright and director named Noda Hideki the harbinger of something very important. I wrote regularly for his Yume no Yuminsha's *PSD Magazine* (Yume no Yuminsha, literally "Idlers' Dream," was the name of his theater company), and praised him as the new voice in Japanese theater in articles in the English-language press, including the *Far East Economic Review*. As with Inoue Hisashi's work, I saw a serious and polemical message in Noda's seemingly nonsensical wordplay.

My worry came not from the playful laughter in contemporary plays but from the giddy prosperity of the decade and the unfettered consumption, blown all out of proportion, of the socalled "new breed" of consumers and their parents.

The *shinjinrui* (new breed) of the 1980s were the first generation of Japanese to have no recollection whatsoever of postwar misery and the first to have a pocketful of money with which to splash out on the fashion, music and new electronic goods they took a fancy to. Their outlook was *neaka* (bright to the core), their reactions spontaneous, based more on immediate emotions than deep contemplation. The manufacturing world loved them and the advertising world adored them. Their trendy effect on Japanese tastes was immense, and it is still felt today in the culture's rejection of its old, deep and meditative nature. The new breed may no longer be new, but their cultural predilections still rule a Japan that has come to be dominated by that MASK phenomenon— manga, anime, sushi and karaoke—all words that have slipped easily from Japanese into the English language and many other foreign languages.

The culture of the 1980s came to be seen as something useful primarily for immediate gratification, not, as in earlier generations, as a thing created for long-term aesthetic pleasure or social good. In short, modern Japan was experiencing its first generation of selfish and, in some senses, healthily self-centered people. Previous generations of men and women had been inculcated in the dogma of personal self-sacrifice. This was no longer applicable. What should you be sacrificing yourself for anyway?

While this shift in cultural orientation created a commercial boom in the 1980s, its greedy side effects, symbolized by the gross actions of the *jiageya* (land price sharks), turned the Japanese economy into an overleveraged nightmare. When the commercial and financial bubbles burst at the beginning of the 1990s, many Japanese again experienced a fall into the inferno, as Sakaguchi Ango had described the postwar ethical void many years earlier, this time not one of physical destruction to the country but of psychological collapse. The postwar model of growth for growth's sake had led to an economic and social bubble that burst, leaving a vast opaque emptiness in front of everyone, chacterized by the Japanese phrase *gori-muchu*, "five miles of fog."

The internationalization of the country in the 1980s was, by and large, genuine. Many Japanese people up to then had had a "foreigner complex." By going overseas themselves in the millions and by listening to foreigners on TV speak fluent Japanese, this complex, like that of poor Toshio, the young man in Nosaka's "America Hijiki," started, thank goodness, to become a thing of the past. But all of this positive trendiness and progressive change came at a cost: the neglect of severe and endemic economic, political and social problems that would emerge full blown in the 1990s and remain with Japan until the present day.

I must confess, though, that while I was worried about the overzealousness of the boom, I personally enjoyed its benefits to the fullest in a cultural sense. Poet Tanikawa Shuntaro introduced me to actor Kishida Kyoko, and I asked her if she would appear in my adaptation of Strindberg's play *Miss Julie*, which I called *Julia*. She graciously said that she would be in it, and this began a collaboration with her not only on *Julia*, which I directed at the

Haiyuza Theater in Roppongi, but also on a play by Witkiewicz, *The Little Manor*, at Parco Part 3 in Shibuya. Hashizume Isao also acted in the Witkiewicz play, and this led to a friendship with him that has lasted to this day. ("Zume" moved into our little attached house at Soshigaya 5-chome when we moved to nearby Seijo; and when their and our children were growing up, we spent many days together with him and his Okinawan wife Yayoi at Kinuta Park and evenings at our home and various restaurants. To me he is the Dustin Hoffman of Japan.)

Kyoko died on December 17, 2006, two days after my mother. Kyoko was seventy-six; my mother, ninety-four. It may sound strange, but I was equally saddened by the two deaths. With Kyoko's passing Japan lost not only a stunning stage presence but also an immense creative spirit and inspiration to young actors.

She had a very subtle and droll sense of humor. To some scenes she brought a lightness, an infectious frivolity. But in other scenes of a play or movie she could produce an intensely concentrated wrath. And what a unique, low and tender voice she had! I will never forget her sublime, easy smile when standing behind the counter offering drinks to Kato Daisuke in Ozu Yasujiro's 1962 film *Sanma no Aji* (*An Autumn Afternoon*). Altogether, the Western actress most like her is probably Jeanne Moreau. As for *Sanma no Aji*, I am lucky to have known three actors from that movie: Kyoko; veteran actor Nakamura Nobuo, who together with her was associated with Theater Troupe En; and Kato Daisuke, who I met decades ago in Kyoto and whose narrative covering his stint in New Guinea during the war, *Snow Falling on the Island in the South*, published in 1961, is, to my mind, a classic in the genre of wartime diaries.

I have myriad memories of meetings with Kishida Kyoko and our work together over the years. She was a painstaking experimentalist during rehearsals. On one run-through of *Julia* not long before opening night I abruptly interrupted the scene. We went into a huddle. I suggested that her line of approach to her character may not be leading to anything fruitful.

"Nevertheless," she said, giving me one of her very cold hard stares, "I am going to pursue it. I need to try everything, Roger-san!"

It was a joy to watch the processes she went through to become her character. After opening night of *Julia* I went backstage and stood behind her holding a potted orchid. She had just removed her makeup and was peering at me in the mirror. She turned around and stood up.

"This is the very same variety of orchid," she said, with a tear in her eye, "that Mishima Yukio gave me the first night of his *Salome*." (She was one of Mishima's favorite actors, and I think, actually, the two of them were in love.)

Kyoko adored children. She produced and acted in an annual Christmas play for children. She loved playing with our little ones when Susan and I took them on visits to her flat in the heart of Roppongi. All in all she acted in more than forty films. One memorable night, she brought director Ichikawa Kon to see *Julia*. After the play the three of us went to a coffee shop behind the Haiyuza Theater in Roppongi.

"I love your use of sound in the play," Ichikawa said to me. "Would you like to do the sound for my next movie?"

I was so flabbergasted I could hardly speak.

"Why... why... yes... yes," I muttered, nodding up and down.

Naturally I never heard from him again.

The last time I saw Kyoko was at Theater X (Cai) in Ryogoku in 2004. She came to see two plays I had written in Japanese and directed. She stayed on, and we chatted in the empty theater.

"My greatest joy now," she said, "comes from my granddaughter. She doesn't call me *obaachan* (grandma), you know. She calls me Kyoko. That's the way I want it."

Forty years elapsed since the time I first saw her on the screen in Los Angeles in *Woman in the Dunes* and that last meeting in an empty Tokyo theater in 2004. In January 2006 she was diagnosed with the brain tumor that took her life at the end of that year.

The 1980s had provided a tall platform from which to look out over Japan and its culture. I was the beneficiary of enormous fortune in getting to know so many creative people. The world celebrates American culture in its brilliant ability to communicate openly; Italian culture with its stylishness; French culture with its studied sophistication. German culture, Russian culture, Chinese culture, Iranian culture, Turkish culture ... every country has a special message for the world. But is there any with the exquisite refinement, the artless elegance and the subtle introspectiveness of Japan?

It was in mid-July 1983 that I met Atsumi Kiyoshi on the set of the thirty-first film in the series of *Otoko wa Tsurai yo* titled *Tora-san's Song of Love*. This series, at forty-eight the longest in film history, directed by Yamada Yoji, was at one time producing nearly 50 percent of the box office revenue for its production company, Shochiku. The set was built in the cavernous Studio 9 at Ofuna outside Tokyo. Walk onto it and you were in a truncated version of Tokyo's traditional downtown area with the Toraya dumpling shop recreated in all its quaint, if shabby, glory.

Atsumi was an actor who could access a tremendous depth of emotion and display it with an almost imperceptible grin, a warmhearted man who talked to me about Japanese compassion and how children in downtown Asakusa used to be scolded by neighbors, affording the place an atmosphere of being one big family.

"Tokyo has changed so drastically," he said while resting between shots. "Nowadays the only thing you know about your neighbors is what brand of beer they drink and what newspaper they take, which you can tell when they put out the garbage."

I became good friends with Tsutsui Yasutaka, a dyed-in-the-wool iconoclast and a staunch voice for freedom of expression in Japan.

"A writer may be the only person," he told me, "who is capable of thinking for society what is truly good and truly evil. I guess I'm a little bit like Sakaguchi Ango, namely, antisocial. What can you do? Society is eaten away by what parades as common sense."

I was fortunate to be able to direct veteran actor Kiyokawa

Nijiko on stage in the Japan premiere of Sam Shepard's Pulitzer Prize-winning play *Buried Child*. It was the first and only modern stage play she ever acted in. Before the war she lived in Soshigaya, which was near the old PCL Studio, now the Toho Studio, where many of Japan's silent classics were produced. I asked her what it had been like to work with Marlon Brando in *The Teahouse of the August Moon*.

"I was his lover, you know," she said, coyly.

"Oh my God, really?"

"That's right, Pulvers-san. We kissed."

"Is that all, just kissed?"

"Yes, that's all."

"Well," I said, glancing around at the others actors, who were riveted to the conversation, "in my country we don't call people who do that lovers."

By 1986 Susan and I had moved from Soshigaya to the neighboring suburb of Seijo where our next-door neighbor was film director Itami Juzo's mother (and also the mother-in-law of author Oe Kenzaburo, who later was awarded the Nobel Prize in Literature). We had a car but had no place to park it, and she had a parking space but no car. She was kind enough to allow us to use her parking space, which was very important to us, having little children. Oe, his wife and son used to pass by our home often on visits to her.

As for Oe, I got to know him quite well after interpreting for him for a speech he gave under the auspices of the Japan Foundation. It was a speech about what in Japanese is called *ika*, which happens to be a homonym for the word for "squid." Luckily I had read the works of Viktor Shklovsky, the Russian writer who had developed the theory of this ika, which in Russian is *ostranienie* (estrangement, distancing, alienation). Otherwise, I would have prepared for the interpreting job by boning up on sushi. Oe lived in Seijo too, and we met from time to time to discuss Japanese literature, particularly the works of our mutual friends, Inoue Hisashi and Kara Juro.

Kara, his wife Li Reisen and their young son (and later actor)

Gitan were frequent visitors at our home for dinner. I love to cook, and created a dish for Kara called "Kara-kuchi Crab," a pun on his name and the word for "spicy." (I wanted to make this when appearing on the TV show *Cuisine Heaven*, but they asked for something Australian, so I cooked lamb marinated in yoghurt instead.) Kara loves children, and I have more than a dozen photos of him holding our children as babies and toddlers over the years.

Like Oe, Yamada Yoji was also in Seijo and had once lived as a struggling young filmmaker not far from our former home in the huge old Soshigaya block of flats called at the time "Culture Housing." Yamada and his wife came to visit not long after our son was born. Though born in Japan, Yamada had grown up in Manchuria where his father was an engineer for Mantetsu, the South Manchuria Railway Company founded in 1906 and controlled by the Empire of Japan until its and the company's demise in 1945. He was sixteen before he returned to Japan. This gave him a very sharp view of what Japan did in China during the war; and I have always enjoyed our discussions about Japan and its wartime responsibility. Yamada's films, by the way, are very popular in China today.

On my thirty-ninth birthday, May 4, 1983, I had invited poet Shiraishi Kazuko for lunch at noon. She still hadn't arrived though it was past 2 pm. I phoned her home but there was no answer. I walked down the shopping street at Soshigaya, thinking she might have lost her way and met her coming out of the station.

"I'm sorry, Pulvers-san," she said, out of breath. "Terayama Shuji died today, and I couldn't make it on time."

Terayama, such a brilliant voice in world theater, had suffered from nephritis since his late teens. I recall him saying at the start of the year 1983, "I just want to last to the end of this year." But his kidneys packed in and he died in May.

In the 1980s I met liberal historian Tsurumi Shunsuke, who had visited Australia when he was sixteen in 1938, popular TV chef Doi Masaru (I interpreted for him on a tour of Australian cooking schools), and philosopher Hidaka Rokuro, about whom more later.

LIKE THE FISH WHO LIVE IN THE DEPTHS

In June 1986 my mentor at the *Mainichi*, editor-in-chief Konishi Akiyuki became *Mainichi Shinbun*'s Washington correspondent, and my new editor at the MDN was not as supportive of the Monday Arts page as Konishi had been. I visited Susan who had just given birth to our third child at the Okura Hospital.

"The work at the paper is not going to be the same," I said.

"Then quit."

"What?"

"I can't bear to see you not doing the kind of work you love."

"But, if I quit we won't have enough money to pay the rent in Seijo. And I'll lose my working visa in November, when it runs out."

"Quit. I believe in you."

Here she was, still weak from childbirth, giving me words of encouragement. I was profoundly moved and stood before her speechless. Her resilience, in bringing up four children in Japan and later in forging her own career, has been, over the years, the primary source of my strength.

I went into the *Mainichi* the next day and tendered my resignation for the end of July.

I remember August 1986 as being a particularly sweltering and muggy month even for the Tokyo summer. I spent the days at home writing and taking our two eldest children on the bicycle to a nearby swimming pool. The money started to run out and, frankly, I was worried. Even if I got a job, there would be no guarantee that I could get a new working visa by November.

And then a phone call came in early September from a producer at Nippon Television. "Could you come to Kojimachi to talk about a possible job?"

"Yes, well I could, but I am rather busy these days. Well, let's see, how about tomorrow? Tomorrow morning?"

I was told that announcer Ida Yumi was to be the first female anchor on the six o'clock evening news and I was offered the job of being a daily commentator on her show. And so I became the first regular foreign commentator on a daily news show, and, miraculously I was given a new three-year visa for it. I had taken a big chance by quitting the *Mainichi*. All achievement incurs risk.

In November 1988 we moved from Tokyo to Kyoto, feeling it would be a better and more manageable city for the children to grow up in. We lived beside Shimogamo Shrine in a flat just up the street from the home of physicist and Nobel laureate Yukawa Hideki. I continued to write books and articles, and from April 1989, commuted every Friday to Tokyo to appear on a new television program, *The Week*, hosted by commentator Sasaki Shin'ya and, then still a newcomer, Azuma Chizuru. Every week we discussed political and social issues in Japan and the world. Among the regulars were two men who were to make a mark on Japanese politics, Masuzoe Yoichi, some years later elected governor of Tokyo, and Kaieda Banri, who became a member of the Diet and, between 2012 and 2014, president of the Democratic Party of Japan.

It was around this time that I met and became close friends with a Japanese actor of great genius, Issey Ogata. I was scripting and directing parts of a documentary on contemporary Japan for CNN, and I felt that Issey, one of the most talented and important representatives of Japanese culture of this era, had to be in it. I subsequently met with him often, both after his live shows at Quest Hall in Harajuku, at the Morita Office that managed him, and at our home in Seijo. I used to go to the Morita Office at Noge, not far from Futako-Tamagawa, and cook lasagne for the Moritas, Issey and their staff. Oh how I enjoyed cooking for all those people! Later, when I needed a place to stay in Tokyo in 1999, the Moritas were kind enough to put me up.

One can look back at a decade, or an era, in any number of ways. It is certain that events and trends in the 1980s changed Japan markedly. Some see it as the era of internationalization, when millions of ordinary Japanese started traveling overseas for the first time, many of them looking back at their country and themselves as Japanese in a different light from before. Others see it as the decade of the asset bubble, where *jiageya*, those land price sharks, made overnight fortunes, eventually leading the descent of their compatriots on a darkened spiral staircase.

But for me the decade of the 1980s was the one in which the subculture of Japan, as represented by people such as author Tsutsui Yasutaka and filmmaker Oshima Nagisa, went mainstream. Had the Japanese not been blinded by the flash of a quick yen, characterized in the phrase *nurete de awa* (like putting your wet hand into a pile of millet), which means making "easy money," and had a genuine internationalization sunk into the national consciousness more deeply, then perhaps the egalitarian values of the subculture might have spread more rapidly. Those values encompassed self-reflection on the brutalities of Japan's militaristic past, tolerance for minorities and their alternative lifestyles, understanding of people with disabilities and how much they can contribute to society, and the recognition that Japanese society needed to realign its priorities in order to benefit women and give opportunities to young people who refused to conform to ways of thinking set way back in the Meiji era.

Oshima Nagisa was fond of quoting something said by a man named Akashi Kaijin. In fact he was so fond of quoting it that for a long time I thought it was Oshima himself who first said it and often attributed it to him when quoting it myself.

Akashi Kaijin was a gifted poet who died at the age of thirty-seven in 1939. This is the same age Miyazawa Kenji was when he died in 1933. Kenji died of tuberculosis. Kaijin had leprosy and wrote extensively about his suffering.

The words of Kaijin that Oshima admired were these ...

If you yourself do not burn like the fish who live in the depths of the sea, there will be no light anywhere.

I know that young people in Japan can take the responsibility for their own country's revival into their hands and hearts and burn like the creative young rebellious people of late Meiji, the Taisho era and the 1960s. It simply requires them to recognize that they cannot rely on their elders for guidance. They will have to produce the light themselves.

As for the very Japanese Pulvers family, in 1990 we bought 300 *tsubo* (a bit more than 10,000 square feet) of land in a beautiful village called Kashiwara and built a big house on it, moving there in February 1991. Kashiwara is in Miyamacho, which is about halfway between Kyoto and the lovely town of Maizuru on the coast of the Sea of Japan. Miyamacho is known for being the place in Japan with the most thatched-roof houses. Not three minutes' walk from our home in Kashiwara was the Ishida House, dating from 1650, designated the oldest continually inhabited farmhouse in Japan. Our own home sat on top of a hill in a clearing, and we looked down on the valley and river below, with a shrine founded, it is said, in the year 645 standing between us and the river.

What a life ... always moving, always seeking something new. Is it adventure? Is it folly? Most people live in one place for years. It must seem strange to them to see someone flitting about like a fragile dragonfly, never resting for long in one place. But to me, you go where your instincts tell you to go. Life is not like crossing an open field. It is more like entering a forest, where the trees present you with a maze of choices. It may be easy to get lost. But if you get through, you find out what is on the other side. There may be lakes that have to be crossed and mountains that have to be climbed. I can't imagine a life for myself without discovering what is on the other side of the forest, beyond the lake, over the mountain.

Here we were, a family of six people, huddled in the basement of our home in Kashiwara, as loud and terrifying lightning and thunder crashed throughout the sky over our home. (Miyama is one of the three most famous places in western Japan for lightning.) Susan was born in Liverpool, U.K. and I in New York, U.S.A. Our four children—Jeremy, Alice, Sophie and Lucy—were born in Japan, but were not Japanese citizens. None of us would be considered "Japanese" by either other Japanese or foreigners. And yet, we all considered ourselves to be on our own home ground.

As we clung to each other in the basement, with the thunder

pounding overhead like drums in a thousand orchestras, we felt that we were, nevertheless, where we belonged.

It is what you feel you are that is important, not what others think you ought to be.

PART TWO

9

BECOMING ACCLIMATIZED TO THE WIND AND THE EARTH

If you look at one of the back pages of a Japanese book that is either a biography of an author or a collection of an author's works, you are likely to see a chronology of their life. There is invariably a pattern to these chronologies.

They start out with the person's birth, perhaps with a word about who their parents were, and then follow the person as they go to school, move to another town, another school. They mention the person's favorite hobbies or books as they take them through middle and high school to university, perhaps some foreign travel, a first job, marriage....

Then the first book comes out. And a second book ... a third. Maybe a second marriage ... and a third ... is squeezed in between publications. But the rest of the chronology is usually a listing of when each book came out, prizes won, and so on.

In other words, the person who began life as an ordinary human being becomes a manufacturer of writings, a person whose life is seen only in connection with what they produce on paper. What, I have often wondered, do these chronologies have to do with the actual life of the person who is their subject? Is there no life for a Japanese writer other than that described in a list of books and prizes?

Maybe Miyazawa Kenji was lucky. He did publish two books during his lifetime, but these were both self-published, paid for with money he earned from teaching and funds given to him by his father. Kenji's chronology reads like that of an ordinary person, one who struggles from one day to the next to determine what his own little place in the world should be.

The real dramas of life are embedded in mundane everyday occurrences: the simple joys of preparing food for family and friends, of putting your baby on your back (we used to strap them onto our back in Japan) and walking down the shopping street to buy groceries, of sitting on a warm day under a tree in a park with a book of poems and letting the book slip gradually out of your fingers as you doze off.

And the tragedies of life, small and big, are no different. A button falls off a shirt or dress, or a tooth from the mouth. You bump your car in a parking lot and wonder where you will get the money to fix the fender. An intimate friend dies, and you wonder how you will ever cope with the loss ... and then, some time later, you are laughing again and thinking of what you want to eat that night or where you will travel that summer.

The primary theme of all life is renewal of absolutely everything in the course of time, in the sweep of culture, history, education and the evolution of personal values ... and the renewal of life itself in the birth of children and grandchildren.

All of our experiences, however personal and intimate, are interlinked with the culture of the country we live in. By culture I mean everything that defines the social climate of the country and people, from their customs and their ways of thinking and talking to what is described by that unique Japanese word *fudo*, written with the characters for "wind" and "earth." We don't have a word for fudo in English. Perhaps "climate" is closest, in the sense that we speak in English of the cultural climate of a country. If you become acclimatized to a place, you can say in Japanese *fudo ni nareru*. I became totally acclimatized to life in Japan. I believed that the culture of Japan could flourish once again and that the world would recognize Japan's contribution to world civilization.

But with the 1990s came a period of doubt and a loss of national self-esteem and hope, first with the bursting of the asset bubble, then with the Great Hanshin Earthquake of January 1995, followed just two months later by the Aum Shinrikyo terrorist attack on the Tokyo subway system.

Of course, people's lives returned to normal. Japanese people still had a massive amount money in the bank, and Japan was still a safe and secure place to live. But how long would that money last if a new paradigm of lifestyle was not created? If the theme of life is renewal, how could Japanese life and culture be renewed? It was bound to take at least a generation or longer—and it already has. The pundits in Japan who spoke, in the early 1990s, of five, "at most ten" years of soul-searching inertia until Japan, by some natural mechanism, bounced back were kidding themselves and all of their listeners. The birthrate started to fall year by year; the suicide rate started to rise year by year. Young people withdrew into themselves. They seemed to be more content showing affection and caring for a little toy called a Tamagotchi, a handheld digital pet, than for another human being.

The politicians and bureaucrats, even the more earnest ones, knew only how to solve the country's problems using the old "tried and true" models. Japanese diligence and perseverance would get the country out of its malaise. Just "refasten your loincloth," as the old and rather crude male-dominated saying went, and you'd be up and running again. Or so the old leaders thought. But it did not happen. The country just sunk deeper into a kind of national depression, which still permeates society today. Despite the success of some pop culture phenomena and the foreign tourist boom (overwhelmingly from other parts of Asia), Japan has, in many ways, become a has-been culture, a country on the wane. The Heisei era that ended in the spring of 2019 lasted for three decades. With a few exceptional highs, its culture can well be described by its name, which can mean "becoming flat."

And yet, the world needs Japanese culture in the broadest sense more than it ever did. But before the world can recognize the vast treasures that reside in this country, Japanese themselves have to recognize them first, learn about them and create ways of communicating and marketing them to the world. Only this will revive the economy and re-energize society.

I think that the term "cultural entrepreneurship" is a crucial one for Japan today. It is one thing to have a great culture, but if you don't know how to entrepreneur and share its riches, it becomes what is called in Japanese *takara no mochi-gusare*, a useless possession, a wasted treasure. This is precisely the term that describes the malaise in Japan today.

What do we in Japan need to recognize in order to jump-start this country, to give it a new burst of energy?

First, we need to recognize that the culture of a country is created by its rebels and misfits. There is no seniority system when it comes to culture. The tools for creating a new Japanese culture—and the reins of power—should be in the hands of young people. The culture of Meiji, with all its faults and, in the end, misguided nationalism, was created by young people who strove to reinvent the Japanese brand.

Second, it is time to think of culture in the same way we think of national defense. I would suggest that Japan adopt a new motto: *Fukoku Kyogei*. In the Meiji era the national motto was *Fukoku Kyohei*. This may be translated as "Enrich the Nation by Strengthening the Military." But if you substitute *gei* (the arts, culture) for *hei* (the military), it becomes: "Enrich the Nation by Strengthening the Culture."

What are the elements of Japanese life and national character, of Japanese culture and behavior that can recreate Japan this century? This is the question I want to address in the succeeding chapters.

10
OVERTURNING THE PAST

Among the many qualities that I have seen in abundance in more than fifty years of living with the Japanese are genuine warmth and innocence. Nothing brings this out more than the Japanese response to children.

Now, you may say, people all over the world are kind to little children. But there is a special quality here which Susan and I experienced almost every day when our children were little.

I noticed it when we were at a park or on a train with the children. Boys of middle school age would come up to them, smile and say, "They're so cute," before starting to talk to them. I have never seen teenage boys in the countries I have lived or traveled in do this so spontaneously and naturally.

In the West people have become wary of any stranger talking to or smiling at their children. In Japan there is a universal affection for children. Even though Atsumi Kiyoshi noted that people don't scold other people's children anymore, there is still a strong feeling that "my child is everyone's child and everyone's child is my child."

The institution of the *boshi techo*, or mother-and-child health record book, is something that should be adopted by other countries. (Indonesia, with help from the Japanese government, introduced the boshi techo in the 1990s; and they are also in use in the Philippines and Palestine, among other countries.) These are issued to women of all nationalities in Japan when they register a pregnancy. They record health issues for both as the pregnancy progresses and the child is born. Though the boshi techo was instituted in Japan in 1942 as a measure to supply a continued source of healthy children for the war effort, it became a wonderful way of tracking and ensuring the health of pregnant women, new mothers and newborn babies. We cherish the four boshi techo that we have from the birth of our children in Japan.

When Susan was pregnant she was grateful for the fact that banks had toilets! In the West, as far as I am aware, you generally cannot use the toilets in a bank. As her tummy got bigger and bigger, there was increasing pressure on her bladder. The old gents who greet people in the bank and help them fill out forms knew exactly why she was stopping off without withdrawing or depositing money and directed her to the right place.

The convenience of life in Japanese cities and towns makes life easier for people who either cannot or do not wish to drive. The area around and near stations in Tokyo comprises a little microcosm of a town, where you can get almost anything you want without traveling far. It means that you can enjoy a kind of village life centered on your station, in the world's biggest metropolis. This provides a kind of warmth of place and a sense of security that you don't get in most big cities of the world.

I conducted a survey in 1983 of all the shops and services on the long shopping street at Soshigaya, compiling what became a very long list of every cake shop, beauty salon, doctor's office, grocery, etc. In 2006 I repeated the survey on the street to compare how the Tokyo lifestyle had changed, publishing the results in a two-part article in the *Japan Times*. It turned out that not much had changed at all, save for the trappings of technology. (Mobile phone stores had popped up where the first video rental shops had been; and the umbrella repair shop had gone with the wind.) The people living in the vicinity of Soshigaya Okura Station had pretty much the same needs and wants they had twenty-three years earlier. Home in Tokyo is the station you live near.

Some people view the Japanese customs of courtesy and politeness as formal and rigid. In many cases, of course, it is no more than a manifestation of perfunctory convention. But there is a considerate aspect to it too, as when people apologize even when something isn't their fault. We in the West are hung up on whose fault something is. If you step on someone's toe in the train, they expect you to apologize. They would generally not apologize for such a thing having been done to them. But wasn't it their toe that went under your foot? This is the way most Japanese people look upon the cause and effect of something accidental. When both sides apologize politely in Japan, a sense of wellbeing and nonconfrontation is created that you don't often see under similar circumstances outside Japan.

Another thing that always struck me is the fact that working people are polite and courteous, as a matter of course, to the general public while on the job. This is certainly not the case across the board in the U.S., Europe, Australia, Russia, China and, I suspect, most other countries. The men and women who direct traffic at a construction site always apologize for causing pedestrians inconvenience. In the West all you can expect is a curt wave of the hand. When I was living at Midoroikecho, I had no flush toilet in my house. The *kumitori* (sewage collecting) men would come with their vacuum truck and empty the tank under the outdoor toilet. Even these men spoke politely to me, often apologizing for the inconvenience they were causing me.

This deferential courtesy is indicative of the cooperative spirit that permeates Japanese society. This cooperative spirit is something that exists in other countries at certain times in their history, such as during a war, but quickly dissolves when it is seen as no longer necessary. When a natural disaster strikes Japan, this cooperative spirit takes over from everything else, and the entire country unites in helping the victims of the disaster get back on their feet again. At such times you see a widespread mood of *jishuku* overtaking the country. Jishuku means "self-restraint, self-discipline." The jishuku displayed by people in Tokyo after the Great East Japan Earthquake disaster struck Tohoku in March 2011 comes, in part, from the feeling that even though you yourself were not a direct victim, you share in the tragedy and show your compassion by refraining from excess yourself. The Japanese are not averse to austerity. In fact when the situation warrants, they wallow in it.

There are many ways that the Japanese cooperative spirit, with its concomitant civic harmony, manifests itself in ordinary times as well. You see it in the phrase *minna no okage*. This means "thanks to everyone." When something good happens to you or you are given credit for an accomplishment, your immediate reaction is to say that it is thanks to others (whether this is true or not). It is taken, needless to say, as a sign of humility. But it is also an element of the cooperative spirit that, whoever may "deserve" the credit for something, credit is best appreciated when it is shared by everyone. This is why there is such an obstacle to adopting a system of meritocratic reward in Japan.

The culture of Japan is not only the tea ceremony and kabuki and the films of Kurosawa Akira and the popular aspects of the MASK phenomenon. It is manifested is small personal gestures that add up to characterize what we call national character, or the nature of a nation. These manifestations are always in flux; and in one era or another the gestures and patterns of behavior that they indicate may all but disappear from the cultural grid. But once they are part of a culture, they do not vanish forever. They can always be revived. And in many cases they should be revived without the old-fashioned and often stultifying customs that accompanied them in the past. It won't do to superimpose "values" from other societies that are founded on very different civic foundations. You've got to reinvent your values from the raw material of your own culture, modified and enriched, as they may be, from the outside.

The Japanese are generally a trusting people, and so, when overseas, they are easily cheated, though over the last decade or two I think they have become more wary. The socalled *ore-ore sagi*, or "It's me, it's me con game," could hardly occur, it seems to me, on such a scale in any other developed country. A man phones an old person, usually a woman, pretending to be their son. He asks for a huge sum of money, sometimes in excess of $100,000, to be sent to his bank account to get him out of some mess he has fallen into. The old person, more often than you would suspect, trots off to the bank and transfers the money without bothering to check with the real son if the request is genuine. This has become so prevalent in

Japan that, for a time, guards stood in many ATM booths to screen possible victims of this scam; and when you now transfer funds on an ATM machine, a notice comes up on the screen asking if you are possibly being cheated. If my parents had ever received a call from someone pretending to be me and asking for money, they would have first quizzed the person about a number of personal things that no one else could know. Dad would have gotten so angry, the hapless conman might have ended up sending money to dad's account to get him off his back.

I think of the personality of Giovanni in Miyazawa Kenji's *Night on the Milky Way Train*. Giovanni is naïve, trusting and easily hurt by unkindness. His personality may be amply described by the Japanese word *kerenminonai*, which combines "unaffected," "unpretentious" and "unworldly" in one. Needless to say, not all Japanese boys are like Giovanni. But this young boy with the Italian name has qualities of warmth, consideration for others and an innocent sense of hope that I think typical of one aspect of the character of the Japanese.

Yet the view of the Japanese in most countries is one of an overly formal, stiff and standoffish, if polite, people. Which brings me to my next discussion of why this gap in perception may exist.

Why is it that the one thing most people around the world agree on—and even some Japanese, too—is that the Japanese lack a rich sense of humor?

Russians and Americans tell jokes all the time to each other. Political jokes. Religious jokes. Jokes about sex. Jokes about ethnic groups (though jokes about ethnic groups other than your own are now out of social bounds). Japanese people generally don't tell jokes to each other. When I meet my Jewish relatives or friends for the first time in a while, we tend to tell each other the latest jokes, many of them actually rehashed old ones. I have never done this with Japanese friends (I don't have any Japanese relatives).

Needless to say, Japanese people do have a sense of humor, but it is oriented to real-life situations. Something comes up in conversation when talking about a person or some incident, and someone makes a funny comment about them or the incident, perhaps using wordplay, so common in Japanese. The Japanese sense of humor creates a mini-comedy of manners. It is part of the drama of experienced life, not humor predicated upon some hypothetical occurrence ("so-and-so walks into a bar"). Inoue Hisashi used to say to me, "Our trouble is that we Japanese laugh and sneer too much at real life. If we took things more seriously, we might start to change them."

If you consider the humor in the works of Ihara Saikaku, the early Edo-period poet and satirist, or look to the stories in kyogen plays, the themes of senryu (comic haiku) or the dialogue in hilarious one-person recited rakugo dramas, you will see how subtle, sophisticated and outrageous the Japanese sense of humor can be. But this sense of humor is always rooted in the customs and manners (or lack of manners) of the people. As such it comprises a genre of social satire when taken together in these various forms.

Japanese humor can have a real anti-authoritarian bite. It is not all the slapstick and nonsense you see on television. There is a dark element in some of the works of modern and contemporary authors that comments trenchantly on the human condition.

Humor pervades the films of Ozu Yasujiro, from his early silent films all the way to his later films like *Tokyo Story, An Autumn Afternoon* and the whimsical and bitter-sweet masterpiece that is my favorite among his films, *Good Morning.* Of course, there is great poignancy and sometimes bitter nostalgia in his films. But these do not negate the comic elements. Ozu's sense of humor is a kind of existential one: Life itself—and the passage of time—is permeated with a sense of absurd and wistful resignation.

Inoue Hisashi's great works of prose and drama treat humanistic themes, and the humor in them is always situational, arising out of the way individual characters interact under the duress of circumstances. In all his work humor is used as a tool by the weak against the strong. Even when the weak do not win, at least what is amusing and comical makes life more tolerable for them and us. If we can laugh at something, we can live through it. In that sense,

OVERTURNING THE PAST

Hisashi's humor is very Jewish.

The Jews have been a perpetual minority wherever they lived (except Israel, which is the single exception in a history spanning more than two thousand years). The main theme of the life of the Jews wherever they lived was survival: how to survive and, if possible, prosper in an essentially hostile environment. The Jews discovered humor as one of their key defense mechanisms. If they could make people from the majority ethnic group laugh, then maybe those people wouldn't persecute or kill them. Of course, it wouldn't do to make up funny stories about your ethnic rulers. They might object and oppress you even more cruelly. So the Jews turned their funny stories on themselves.

The main thrust of Jewish humor became self-deprecation. Jews told funny stories and jokes about how miserly they themselves were, about how stupid, how narrow minded, how behind the times they were. And everyone laughed, Jews and nonJews alike. Three or four generations of Jewish comedians in the United States, from Molly Picon to Gertrude Berg, from the Marx Brothers to Jack Benny, from Mel Brooks to Lenny Bruce, from Danny Kaye to Woody Allen, Jerry Seinfeld and Sarah Silverman, and literally scores more who made an impact on American entertainment and life, come out of this tradition. The role of this humor is to help others understand you. Your survival depends on strangers recognizing you as a human being or, as the old Jewish saying goes, "just like everyone else, only more so."

The Japanese, on the other hand, have been the dominant ethnic group in this country since the beginning of history. There is no need for them to have to explain themselves to others who might destroy them. The universal approach has been the opposite of that of the Jews: No one can understand you anyway so why try? Perhaps you even get a bit more mystery about yourself, a kind of aura, if you appear inscrutable. *Not* explaining yourself gives you power. *Haragei*, which literally means "belly art" but translates as "communicating silently through the force of personality," is the farthest thing you can get from a belly laugh.

When I think of my friend Issey Ogata, it occurs to me that this man could have become world famous in the world of entertainment and acting had he been born in a country whose language was more well known in the world. Issey is on par in his genius for social parody with great Jewish comedians like Groucho Marx, Jerry Lewis and the Jewish British comedian, Sacha Baron Cohen.

Issey's humor is quintessentially self-deprecating. He creates characters, both men and women, who are ultra-typical Japanese, who display all of the foibles, shortcomings and recognizable gestures of Japanese people. In both his live shows and his DVDs, he recreates the face of the Japanese nation. There is often a black existential humor in his performances, as when a salaryman gets lost in a parking lot and he can't tell if the name cards in his pocket are his own or someone else's.

The main reason why the Japanese are thought to have little sense of humor stems from the fact that humor doesn't play much of a part in public life. Work is work, and, as the Japanese phrase goes, "This is no place for joking." Sadly that phrase is used anywhere where serious intent is called for. There's no way to break the ice. In other words, in Japan there is a time and a place for humor, and that time and place are largely limited to encounters in private or in the entertainment media. In many other countries all times and all places are suitable for humor. A politician can crack a joke even when the atmosphere is very grave. An executive can drop a funny comment in a serious meeting. A priest or pastor can joke during a church service. You can be droll at a funeral (and may even be expected to be), or pleasantly sarcastic when discussing your affairs at a government office. In Japan making comic remarks at the "wrong time" goes against the decorous manner of society. *Four Weddings and a Funeral* would have been called *Four Weddings but not at the Funeral* in Japan. This is why Japanese appear so humorless in many public situations. Humor is out of place there.

But the wit, irony, satire and general sense of fun that we see throughout all Japanese history, particularly that which abounded in the Edo period, is something that the world should get to know. (The works of Hokusai best represent this.) Japanese humor is subtle and grounded in everyday occurrences, and has been for centuries.

And, as with Ozu's films, so it is with some of the haiku of a great poetic genius. There can be a touching wistfulness to Japanese humor …

It's drizzling outside
As the the cold lump of jelly
Slides down my belly

This is a haiku by one of the most brilliant and radical poets of the modern era, Masaoka Shiki, a man who spent years in a sickbed and died in 1902 at the age of thirty-two.

Shiki had put *konnyaku* on his stomach as a kind of natural hot water bottle so that the warmth would ease his pain. Konnyaku is a common jelly-like food in Japan made from the root of an Asian plant resembling a lily. It retains heat when warmed. But as a light rain of summer fell, so did the temperature of the air, and poor Shiki is left with a big useless cold lump of konnyaku sitting on his belly, a symbol of his inert life in bed. This is a poignant and somewhat comical metaphor of life, illness and, perhaps, an omen of death.

Shiki's sarcasm reached out to the greatest haiku master of them all, Basho, whose classic haiku about a frog was borrowed, revived and turned on its back by him …

First, Basho's classic …

An old pond
A frog plunges
In a splash

Now, Shiki's retort …

That old pond
And on it floats a cicada's shell
Upside down

Despite their very different histories, maybe the Jews and the Japanese do have something in common. We both see ourselves as misunderstood and do our best to overturn the past in order to keep it, and ourselves, alive.

11

A LABYRINTH OF COLOR

Japan is a theatrical country.

In the theater everything is a gesture: hand and body movements, voice, facial expression. Some gestures may be representational, that is, they mimic gestures found off the stage; other gestures may be stylized and abstract, only suggesting movement and tone of voice in real life, yet giving us insight into how those gestures are made and what their emotional meaning is.

A young man walks across the stage, goes up to a woman, who is playing his granny, and hugs her. A Western actor will ask himself, "What is my motivation for this?" He may find that the character in the play does not love his granny at all. The actor has to find some psychological motivation as an actor playing that character in order to walk to his granny and hug her. Until he discovers and accesses it in himself, he finds it hard to make this gesture convincingly. It will look artificial and forced.

A Japanese actor may not be so worried about this psychological motivation in the very beginning. He will walk to his granny and hug her. He will do the gesture with as much skill and technique as he can muster. Again, at first, the gesture may look forced. But he is called upon to do it by his role, so he does it.

Gradually the Western actor will find some motivation in himself. Even though the character he is playing doesn't love his granny, she is after all an old helpless woman. She deserves pity. The Japanese actor will, after practicing the gesture of walking to her and hugging her over and over again, get very good at it. By "good" I mean skillful; he will look like a real human being performing a real human action. The motivation can well up in him while he is hugging her. The important thing is the action itself. The emotion fills the vessel of the action while the action is being done. In the

West, most actors feel they have to experience the emotion before they can perform the action.

Please excuse this long and seemingly theoretical explanation. But it bears significantly, to my mind, on the everyday gestures of Japanese people in real life. When I wrote that Japan is a theatrical country, I was referring to the gestures and conventions of everyday life.

We often start a Japanese email or a telephone conversation to someone in Japan with "I am deeply indebted to you" even when we may not really be in their debt. When you enter a restaurant you may hear everyone working in it, from the waiters and waitresses to the chefs behind the counter, yell "Welcome!" and when you leave, "Thank you very much!" When you receive something formally, such as a diploma at a graduation ceremony, you bow while holding up the diploma in both hands, generally raising it above your head. At other times you bow to different people in different ways and on different angles, depending on the formality or informality of the relationship. Even many beautiful ancient Buddhist statues have one hand raised and one palm open in front of them, the latter in a gesture of openness and generosity. These gestures are gestures of everyday theatricality.

Japanese articles of clothing can be theatrical too. I think of the *hachimaki* (headband) and what it represents to Japanese people. There is a restaurant chain called Ganko (Stubborn) whose logo is a man with a stern expression on his face and a tightly tied hachimaki. It would be unthinkable for there to be a popular restaurant in the West called "Stubborn" featuring such a grumpy man as its symbol.

The word *urusai* has very negative usages. "Urusai!" is the equivalent in English of "Shut up!" But if someone is urusai in terms of taste, we generally conjure the image of a gourmet. The Ganko logo is Japanese theatricality at its most effective, picturing a chef who is urusai (particular, hard to please). But then again, this may be a case not of Japanese theatricality but rather of Osaka theatricality, for that is where the restaurant chain Ganko began, in a little sushi shop in 1963.

I had two experiences, one in the 1970s and the other in the '80s, that taught me just how theatrical the Japanese can be. The first was with the great noh actor Kanze Hisao. I have never seen an actor of such brilliance on the noh stage as Kanze Hisao. The way he stood, leaned forward holding a pose, danced and used his masks to such subtle levels of expression was astounding. I saw him in 1975 in *Aoi no Ue* (*Lady Aoi*, based on an episode in *The Tale of Genji*) at Tokyo's Mitsukoshi Theater, and some years before then at Kanze Kaikan in Kyoto in W. B. Yeats's play adapted for the noh stage, *At the Hawk's Well*.

Kanze told me in January 1976 that he wanted to revive the spirit of Zeami (playwright and actor active in the early fifteenth century), where truth is something demonstrated in an instant of inspired revelation, and *yugen*, or profound subtlety, lingers in the air. "That's what the set forms and styles of performance are for, not vice versa like now," he said, "when the forms and styles are performed perfunctorily." I asked him if he wanted to take noh back to the spirit of Zeami, but he answered that he was taking noh forward to the spirit of Zeami by making it once again a flexible creative force. He was to me the incarnation of everything that Zeami strove to express in using the ritual of total theater—word, dance, music, costume, mask—in a perfectly integrated form, the epitome of the Japanese dramatic gift.

I met Kanze Hisao a number of times while attending rehearsals of a play he was in directed by Suzuki Tadashi, and went up to Togamura in Toyama prefecture in 1975 to see him act in it. But the most wonderful time we spent together came after I received a telephone call from him that year out of the blue.

"Hello, Pulvers-san? This is Kanze. Could you please come tomorrow to the Tessenkai in Omotesando?"

"Of course. I would love to. Is there a noh performance tomorrow?"

"Well, please come anyway. At noon."

I arrived at the old Tessenkai Theater near Omotesando Station the next day not knowing what I was going to see. I entered the deserted entry hall and called out to him. No one came. Had I understood him correctly, I wondered. Maybe he had specified another day or time. Where were the other members of the audience? Again I called out to him, this time in a louder voice.

Kanze appeared out of the dark corridor, greeted me and said, "Please, this way."

I followed him into the empty theater. I had expected at least some other people to be there, but there was no one but the two of us.

"This is what I wanted you to see," he said, pointing to the stage.

On stage were dozens of colorful kimonos used in the noh. This was an airing out of the theater's costumes, and he had brought me there to view them.

"Please, this way," he said again, stepping onto the stage.

Again I followed. As he wove his way around each kimono I lost sight of him. It was as if I was following him through a labyrinth of spectacular color and textures, his arm or hand or leg or shoulder suddenly visible, then gone; a soft silky sleeve of a kimono woven hundreds of years ago brushing against my cheek.

I suppose that we were inside that maze of color for only two or three minutes. But, as in the noh play *Kantan*, where a man at an inn takes a nap and lives decades of his life in grand splendor, only to wake up a few minutes later, this short interval of time seemed to last for an age. When I stepped back down off the stage and faced him I felt as if I had been on a journey in space and time. Kanze Hisao had, by weaving his way among the kimonos above the noh stage, redesigned time itself for me. The experience was like living in a noh play; and after that I understood the spirit of noh much more deeply. Kanze Hisao's untimely death in 1978 from stomach cancer crushed me. He was only fifty-three. (Not long after that day, I went again to the theater to see a noh play. I sat in my chair long after the rest of the audience had gone. I noticed a woman walking slowly from one row to another, lifting all the seats back to the upright position. It was actress Seki Hiroko, who I had met on a number of occasions. She was Kanze Hisao's wife. My eyes welled with tears watching her go from row to row simply lifting seats.)

The second theatrical experience came in the late 1980s when Susan, the children and I were living at Izumikawacho in Shimogamo, adjacent to the sacred grove of trees in the Shimogamo Shrine called "Tadasu no Mori." Not far from there, up Shimogamo Boulevard, lived one of the great old teachers of tea at Urasenke, a man who I believed to be then in his seventies. This man understood the *kokoro*, or true heart, of tea profoundly and exquisitely.

Susan had studied the tea ceremony at Urasenke in 1980 and had met him then. He was kind enough to invite us to his home for a ceremony.

His wife, also no doubt in her seventies, greeted us formally in the entry hall, bowing on her knees with three fingers of each hand touching in the traditional Kyoto style, before leading us into the ordinary Western-style living room. We sat on a sofa as she disappeared into another room.

After a moment or two we heard Edith Piaf singing *Non, je ne regrette rien*, and out he came, rushing through the doorway dressed in a flowing pink and white chiffon dress, his face made up with lipstick and rouge, his head covered in a flowing brunette wig. He proceeded to do a tea ceremony right there in the living room, with Piaf continuing on in a medley of songs. Not only was it the most theatrical and stunning tea ceremony I have ever attended, it was a tea ceremony that captured fully the kokoro of tea.

What is Japanese theatricality in life? Is it conventions of behavior that have been stylized in language and movement? Is it social ritual that holds this society together, that allows Japanese people to recognize each other and feel at home with each other—a kind of glue of interconnectedness? It is all of these things.

I know as a nonJapanese who has been in Japan since 1967 that living in Japan and speaking Japanese is not just a matter of going about your merry business and using correct grammar. The codes of this society are clear for anyone to see. Japanese people are happy to accept foreigners so long as they follow the Japanese codes of behavior. Those foreigners living in Japan who realize this and follow these unwritten rules usually succeed and find happiness. Those foreigners who cannot give up their own set ways and modes of communication run the risk of forever being outsiders.

As for me, like Lafcadio Hearn, I never considered the mores and customs of behavior of my country or my ethnic group as a standard. If I was going to live in Japan, I was going to live a Japanese life. Of course I was going to do this without giving up my individuality. Many people think of their individuality as being linked to the standards of behavior of the country of their birth, what they consider to be "normal." For me, individuality—and originality and creativity and personal freedom—are inner qualities. They can be cherished and nurtured even when following the codes that Japanese people cherish.

This was brought home to me very early on in my Japanese life.

Not long after coming to Japan and learning to speak Japanese I began to meet many different kinds of Japanese people. Almost all of them asked the same question: "Where did you go to university?"

When I said that I had gone to graduate school at Harvard, they invariably responded with "Oh, wow!" or "Oh my God!" Harvard is even more highly thought of in Japan than in the United States. This attitude is part of the brand consciousness that has existed in this country for centuries.

I naturally strove to avoid this overreaction, so I gradually began to give this answer.

"University? Well, uh, you see, I mean, actually … uh, it wasn't really … that is, I don't mean to, you know … but, well, in a way … it was … I mean, Harvard, but I don't mean to …."

After this very Japanese-style answer, most people responded calmly with "Oh, I see" or "Uh-huh," and that was the end of it.

Was I being Japanese? Not really. I was just speaking in a manner that Japanese people use when communicating with each other. I suppose that such a way of answering this question, especially with the "but I don't mean to" at the end, signals modesty or humility.

I was communicating to people that I personally didn't consider it such a big deal that I went to Harvard, which, in any case, was absolutely true. But were I speaking English it would be ridiculous to answer this question in such a circuitous and seemingly mealy-mouthed manner. The most natural thing would be simply to say in a matter of fact way, "I went to Harvard."

Needless to say, just because a Japanese answers such a question in what appears to be a modest fashion, it does not mean that the person is actually modest. These are the trappings of modesty, the ways in which modesty is signaled in Japanese. These are the codes of behavior, the theatrical rules of social action.

When you speak a foreign language you become, to a certain extent, a different person, but only on the outside. You can retain your individuality and personal conscience no matter how strictly you conform to social codes on the outside.

As for me, over the years this Japanese theatricality has seeped into my inner self and in some ways I act like a Japanese even when I am overseas. Of course, it is natural for expatriates of long standing in any country to assimilate in this way.

In 2000, I had the chance to meet an influential Hollywood agent in Los Angeles. The agent system in America doesn't really exist here like it does in the U.S., where agents are all-powerful. They are the ones who control access to producers in film and theater, publishers and just about any cultural entrepreneur.

This Hollywood agent asked me what I was writing.

"Well," I said, mumbling and looking away from her, "I, uh, well, actually, you see, I mean, it's not really anything ... but I just felt that, you know, I could, if given the chance, write something for a film...."

"You mean a film script?" she said, staring me impatiently straight in the face.

"Film script? Well, uh, yes, I guess, but I...."

It wasn't long before I was rushed out of the office. She must have thought, "What a strangely diffident man that is!"

Actually I am a far cry from being diffident. And I really wanted to write a film script. But I lost my chance forever.

I was simply too Japanese to know how to seize the Hollywood moment and make it happen.

12

THE NATURE OF THE JAPANESE

All over the world, from India to the U.S., from Mongolia to Chile, from Russia to Nigeria and New Zealand, people saw the amazing resilience and orderly behavior of the Japanese in the aftermath of the unprecedented disaster that struck Tohoku on March 11, 2011. Even people who were not well disposed to Japan and the Japanese, such as the Chinese and Koreans, displayed a turnabout, if temporary, in attitude.

The inner strength and fortitude of the people of the stricken districts were remarkable. But something else struck me at that time: the utter selflessness of the victims. They turned their grief into compassion and mercy for others who had lost loved ones. It is no wonder that Kenji's poem "Strong in the Rain," with its message of selfless empathy, is the most popular and beloved poem of modern Japan. After all, this was the poet who wrote, "Personal happiness cannot exist until the whole world is happy."

This quality of selfless empathy was amply demonstrated by the survivors of the Great East Japan Earthquake of 2011. Of course, there are many selfish and self-serving people in Japan. But the motto "Every man for himself" played no part in the tragedy's aftermath. The motto of the people of Tohoku might be: "Every person for every other."

Where does this selflessness come from? Just because a child is born in Japan, it doesn't mean they inherit selflessness. Selflessness is not genetic; it is not in the DNA. The answer is that it comes from being brought up in Japan. It is in the cultural climate here, where deference and compromise are the basis of social harmony.

How does this selflessness or altruism express itself in everyday life? It goes without saying that many people act in heroic (and some in un-heroic) ways in times of crises. But most of us live our life in a mundane routine. We don't experience great crises. In crises as well as in ordinary everyday life, Japanese people are primarily concerned about not causing *meiwaku*, or annoyance, to other people, going to great pains to not be a nuisance to others.

When I was directing Sam Shepard's play *Buried Child* in Shibuya back in the mid-1980s, something happened during the rehearsal period that made me realize how this selflessness manifests itself.

Buried Child takes place on a remote farm in the American Midwest. One day Vince, who has been away for a long time, visits his grandparents on the farm. He takes along his spunky girlfriend Shelly, who has never met the grandparents. Vince and Shelly enter the house to find grandpa sitting on the sofa. Vince goes up the stairs, leaving Shelly alone to deal with a very cantankerous eccentric grandpa.

Shelly introduces herself as Vince's girlfriend and tries her best to be amiable. But grandpa is in a huff for no apparent reason. He refuses to speak to her. At one point Shelly, sitting on the arm of the sofa, thinks she might have said something rude or irritating to him, for, despite her efforts, he remains grumpy and tight lipped. She apologizes to him and asks that he not think ill of her.

When saying this apologetic dialogue, the actor playing Shelly, Tomizawa Ako, stood up from the arm of the sofa and stepped backward a few steps, bowing her head and holding her hands together in front of her. Tomizawa is a superb actor. (She is the daughter of Asakura Setsu, who designed that play and others I directed in Tokyo. Sadly we lost Setsu, Japan's greatest set designer, in 2014, age ninety-one.) The movement during this important moment of confrontation between grandpa and Shelly had to be convincing. But it was wrong.

It was wrong because this play takes place in the Midwest of America, not in Japan. A young spunky American girl would not retreat if she thought she had caused someone irritation. She would move forward. She would sit next to grandpa and perhaps put her hand on his knee, saying, "I didn't mean to upset you. I'm sorry."

Moving toward the person and even touching them is a gesture of

THE NATURE OF THE JAPANESE

reassurance. Shelly is trying to reassure grandpa that she means no harm to him. In Japan a sudden move forward at such a time might be taken as an act of further irritation, even, if misunderstood, aggression. By negating yourself, by making yourself smaller, by moving away and taking yourself away from the center, you indicate apology and remorse. This is one way in which you show selflessness, that you are not the center of attention.

Now that the world has seen how altruistic the Japanese people can be, perhaps people in other countries will attempt to imitate them. If Americans had acted like this after the disaster of Hurricane Katrina that struck New Orleans in 2005, perhaps there would not have been the me-too selfishness, looting and violence that was seen in its aftermath.

Another facet of Japanese selflessness is reticence. This is a quality that some Japanese take to a fault, often making it hard to find out what they are trying to say and what they want. Japanese are known all over the world for being inarticulate. This is fine when Japanese people are speaking to other Japanese people. But, when communicating with people from other countries, the Japanese people are going to have to learn to be more self-assertive and articulate their hopes and desires. I wish I had realized that when I met the agent in Hollywood.

On the other hand, thanks to this culture of inarticulateness, foreigners learning to speak Japanese have it easy. You can mumble and pause. You can speak only in fragments of words, and no one will know you don't speak the language very well. In many situations, broken Japanese is fluent Japanese.

When I first came to Japan I still spoke English in Japanese, that is, I translated what I wanted to say from English to Japanese, as most beginners do in any foreign language. Then, after a while, I realized that I could express myself quite persuasively by using just a few well-chosen words. When a Japanese acquaintance asked me at a party where my wife was, instead of giving an explanation I said, "Well, my wife is actually ..." and leave it at that. This would elicit an immediate response like "Oh, I see!" When asked by another acquaintance why I liked Japan, instead of offering long-winded reasons, I would say, "Well, I just somehow...." The acquaintance would nod knowingly, "Oh, is that so!" Such replies in English might be considered evasive and well might give rise to suspicions of prevarication.

I had another experience which taught me that being "a person of few words" is not only a virtue but can put you at an advantage. In this case it was "a child of few words."

At the beginning of 1992, after living about a year in Kashiwara, Susan and I sold our beautiful country house and moved to Sydney. The children were speaking Japanese—or more specifically, Kyoto dialect—among themselves. Their command of English was not proficient. Though we had tried to teach them to read English by using teaching aids and books we had sent over from Britain, we realized that they would need schooling in English if they were ever to become native speakers.

We had never lived in Sydney before and ended up staying there until December 1994, nearly three years. Susan set up her own business exporting Australian medical supplies and transferring medical know-how to Japan, particularly as that know-how related to the care of patients with Alzheimer's disease. I stayed at home in the lovely bayside suburb of Mosman and wrote. She made fourteen trips to Japan during this time. I must admit I loved being a house husband and looking after the children, who were then between ages of about ten and four. It was one of the happiest times of my life.

But in December 1994 we decided to return to Japan. We lived in Tokyo for a year before moving to Kyoto. When we arrived in Kyoto we had to find a kindergarten that would take our youngest child, Lucy. Susan was still running her business, and I had become a fulltime professor. But the kindergarten wouldn't admit a child who did not speak Japanese; and among our children, Lucy, who had been only two and a half when we left Japan in 1992, was the only one who couldn't.

Well, Lucy's father, namely me, had once written a tongue-in-

THE NATURE OF THE JAPANESE

cheek article called "Five Words to Fluency," claiming that you needed only five words in Japanese to appear fluent in the language. I figured out a way for Lucy to get through the kindergarten interview using only a single word.

"Lucy, I want you to say *hai* (yes)."

"Hai."

"Good. Say it in a confident, sort of a clipped way. HAI!"

"HAI!"

"Good. Now smile when you say it."

"HAI! HAI!"

"Wonderful. Now, during the interview you will be sitting on daddy's lap. Every time daddy pinches your bottom, say hai. Got it?"

"HAI! HAI!"

When the time for the interview came, I was the one who was nervous. I wasn't sure my monosyllabic subterfuge would go as planned.

We walked into the "oral examination room" at the kindergarten holding hands. The principal, an elderly gent, and two female teachers were sitting at a long table facing our single folding chair. I sat on the chair and put Lucy on my lap. The principal spoke first.

"*Konnichiwa* (Hello)."

"Konnichiwa," I said.

Lucy was silent. The principal spoke again, this time to Lucy.

"Lucy?"

I pinched her bottom.

"HAI!"

"Lucy, *nihongo wakaru no* (Do you understand Japanese)?"

Pinch.

"HAI!"

"*Hoikuen ni hairitai* (Do you want to enter the kindergarten)?"

Pinch. Pinch.

"HAI! HAI!"

"*Aa, nihongo ga ojozu desu ne* (Oh, you speak such good Japanese)."

I inadvertently pinched her bottom again.

"HAI!"

Everyone laughed ... and Lucy got into kindergarten.

Japanese definitely do not like people who strive too assiduously to make explanatory excuses. You are much better off if you simply say nothing and bow your head. One word that describes this trait very well is "self-effacement." Being self-effacing, that is, reserved, reticent and avoiding being conspicuous, is a feature of Japanese selflessness, like my Japanese Shelly, retreating, making herself smaller and taking herself out of the center of the picture so as not to cause meiwaku—annoyance, trouble, inconvenience—to other people.

There are countless phrases in Japanese that indicate humility, and these are used with much greater frequency than they are, for instance, in the European languages that I know. "I don't mean to sound like I'm boasting but ... I will do what little I can ... I apologize for not knowing, but I would like to ask you...." These set phrases often precede or appear in the middle of a conversation. It is common for people to begin a public speech, for instance, when being given an award, with something like "That someone like me would appear in front of an august body of people such as you ... I am certainly undeserving of such an honor...." In other words, it is proper to set the tone by apologizing for yourself and your unworthiness. If you used such phrases of humility in most Western countries in an acceptance speech for an award, people might consider you unduly unctuous or come to believe you didn't really deserve it.

The most disliked type of person in Japan is the braggart. Even acknowledging credit for a personal achievement can be seen as bragging. It is always better to be modest about your achievements and let other people brag for you, denying all praise that is bestowed upon you. Of course, if you overdo the humility, people become suspicious. "Belittling yourself excessively is a sure sign of conceit" is a Japanese proverb that speaks of wariness toward people who are insistently self-effacing.

THE NATURE OF THE JAPANESE

Enryo, or reserve, is a well-known quality of the Japanese, and it is related to the traits of self-effacement I have written about above. The word *enryogachi*, literally "a tendency toward reserve," means not only "reservedly" but also "modestly" and "humbly."

Sometimes, however, the situation does not call for reserve and reticence, and a person is required to state an opinion or openly express a desire that may be taken as an infringement on someone else's freedom. How do Japanese manage to do this while still retaining the harmony of an encounter?

Many years ago, when I was working at the *Mainichi Daily News*, one of my coworkers was an American woman who had lived a long time in Japan and spoke excellent, if accented, Japanese. But she was unhappy in Japan and eventually went back to live in New England. The reason why she was unhappy was not that she disliked Japanese people. On the contrary she had many Japanese friends. It was because she never came to realize that she was living in a country where people expressed themselves differently from people in the United States. She just couldn't get used to the social conventions here that are so different from those in her native country.

Here's an example of how the problem manifested itself.

Until the 1990s Japanese smokers would light up just about anywhere—in trains, offices, schools, restaurants—without considering the welfare of the people around them. Japan was a smokers' paradise in which nearly two-thirds of men smoked. (Today the rate is just over one-fourth, and less than one-tenth for women.) My American friend from the *Mainichi* hated cigarette smoke and tried to avoid smokers wherever she went.

One day she came into the newspaper fuming.

"What's the matter?" I asked.

"I just had this awful experience."

"Oh dear."

"This awful man standing right beside me on the platform lit up his cigarette, and the smoke went right in my face."

"You should have just moved away," I said. (My reactions had come to be similar to those of my Japanese Shelly, stepping away from confrontation.)

"Moved away? Why? Why should I move away? He was the one who was smoking."

"So, what did you do?"

"I asked him to stop smoking."

"Well, did he put out his cigarette?"

"No. He just stared at me as if he didn't understand a word I had said."

"Well, what did you say to him? Maybe you made a mistake in Japanese."

"I didn't, Roger! I told him plainly. I said, 'Will you please smoke so that the smoke goes in the other direction.' I even used formal language."

What she had said to the man was in grammatically correct and polite Japanese. Yet the man didn't seem to understand her. If he had, he might have considered her pushy.

So, what was wrong with what she said to the smoker? The problem was that it was an abrupt request aimed directly at him. This is what I told her.

"You should have said, 'Excuse me, but I can't take cigarette smoke.' This would have focused the attention on your own weakness, and he might have responded by apologizing and putting out his cigarette."

"Why should I apologize? He's the one who should apologize for spreading smoke all over the place. It's not my fault!"

Ah, I thought, there's the rub. We Westerners are too often hung up on our own stance: It's not *my* fault. The Japanese are not concerned with whose fault it is. They just want to resolve the problem as harmoniously as possible. And the best way to resolve things harmoniously is for both sides to be humble or, if possible, self-effacing. This is why I mentioned deference and compromise. My American friend should have expressed herself in a self-effacing manner in Japanese, giving some ground, giving the man some leeway; and perhaps this might have moved him to put out

THE NATURE OF THE JAPANESE

his cigarette.

When asked by nonJapanese people if there is a single word that characterizes the Japanese, I say "non-confrontational." Japanese people will go to great pains to avoid unpleasant confrontations, even at the expense of the truth of the encounter or of determining who is "right" and who is "wrong."

The kind of humility in which one shifts the blame to oneself in making a request is a very Japanese trait, and it manifests itself in many modes of behavior, including those that stress sensitivity to the needs and interests of others above your own.

Then there is the consideration of a treasured moment. The lovely phrase *ichigo-ichie* expresses a special sensitivity to a particular person's needs and predilections. This phrase originated in the tea ceremony. It underscores the temporal but precious nature of a single encounter. It means: "Each encounter is to be cherished, for you never know if or when it will ever come your way again."

You go to a friend's home and are served food on a plate that the host thinks you particularly would like. Beneath the culture of Japanese service is the notion that all efforts must be made to please the other person. When a woman has a baby, she naturally receives baby clothes from friends. Many months or even years later, the mother dresses the baby or toddler in those clothes given by the friends who visit. Susan received many wonderful gifts of clothes from our Japanese friends when the babies were born, and she always remembered to dress the children in them when we met those friends again. Unlike my colleague at the *Mainichi*, Susan fit in perfectly in Japan and loved living here. Even though the context was different, she didn't think she was compromising her individuality by "acting Japanese."

The trait of avoiding the appearance of brash self-assertiveness shows up in many other ways in Japan. Virtually every foreign teacher in Japan remarks on the fact that Japanese students don't ask questions in class. I taught for a total of twenty-two years at Japanese universities, and I cannot recall more than a few dozen occasions when Japanese students asked questions in class. About

10 percent of the student body at Tokyo Institute of Technology, where I taught the longest, was foreign. When a hand was raised in class it was almost always a Chinese, Vietnamese, Korean or European one. Then, after class, Japanese students would come up to the front and pepper me with questions while I was erasing the blackboard. They were too embarrassed to ask questions in class because they did not want to appear assertive or challenging.

The *taidan*, or two-person discussion that is so common in Japanese magazines and newspapers, presents another example how this trait manifests itself. Even though the *tai* of taidan means "against," and even though these taidan often carry the headline "Ms. X vs. Mr. Y," taidan are conducted with two people who essentially agree with each other on most things. It is very rare for one to read a taidan between two people who cannot find common ground. Such a confrontational article would cause ill will and reflect badly on the reputation of the publisher.

The key to the success of a Japanese taidan is this common ground. They always begin very amiably. Ms. X praises Mr. Y for something he wrote or said, and Mr. Y avers with a string of ultra-humble clichés. If Mr. Y praises Ms. X for winning some literary prize, Ms. X says, "Oh no, I was so surprised when I won it and surely don't deserve it."

When Ms. X expresses an opinion about something, Mr. Y's first reaction is, "Oh, I see. Yes I agree with you." Whether he agrees or not, this is what he says. Eventually, however, he will add, "But, please consider this," and go on to express his own opinion, which will probably differ in one way or another from hers. The degree of deference they pay each other can be seen in how many nice things they say about each other before they say "But" and state how they really feel. I would hate to have to interpret for any taidan. A good portion of what is said is just a pouring out of self-effacing clichés.

All of this brings me to one of the most enviable features of Japanese life and one that should be understood, imitated and institutionalized in all countries of the world. I am speaking of the culture of service.

THE NATURE OF THE JAPANESE

I am not the first person by any means to say that service in Japan is the best in the world. Japanese people should be going all over the world teaching people how to serve others politely and efficiently.

Japan's culture of courtesy and service is, without doubt, one of the national treasures of this country. The difference between the service culture here and that elsewhere was brought home to me in 2007, when I made one of my monthly trips to Sydney and back to Tokyo. Of course, I am reminded of the vast differences every time I ask a question in a supermarket or store in virtually any city outside Japan.

Most readers will be familiar with the regulations regarding liquids, gels and aerosols in carry-on luggage at airports. I was familiar with them, too, but mistakenly assumed that they didn't apply to liquor. After all, they had only been in force for a short time then. I had bought two bottles of liquor in Tokyo and put them in my carry-on bag.

As you can guess, after my bag went through the X-ray machine, the Japanese customs officials, two young women, asked me to open it.

"What are these bottles?" one asked.

"Oh, this is just liquor."

"I'm sorry," they said, "these cannot be taken on board the plane."

"Oh dear, I'm sorry," I said. "I didn't know."

Then one of the young women smiled.

"Look, you still have time. Why don't you take these bottles out of security and check them? Then it will be fine."

I always traveled back and forth to Sydney without checked luggage and didn't want to be held up on arrival.

"That's very kind of you," I said. "But I'll leave the bottles here."

The other young woman looked at me sympathetically.

"Oh, it's a real shame! I'm sorry," she said.

All in all, I was the one at fault; and, though losing the two bottles, I actually went on to passport control with a good feeling about this, if you will, sobering experience. The customs official had actually apologized to me.

Now for the unpleasant round trip to this story.

Going through the security check at Sydney airport on my way back I thought I was well within the regulations this time, with two little jars of food in my carry-on bag, neither of them containing a liquid. One had dried tomatoes; the other, shredded pickled beetroot. I was taking these to Tokyo to use for a dinner I was to cook at the Nakarokugo home of my friend, that brilliant translator and author, Shibata Motoyuki.

At Sydney airport I was again asked to open my bag. This time, a young woman and young man did the checking. The woman held up the jars and, with a look of disdain, said, "You can't take these on the plane!"

"Oh my gosh," I said, "I'm really sorry. I thought it was OK, because they were..."

"Well, they're not OK!" she said, plonking the jars on the counter.

The young man picked up the jar of pickled beetroot, shook his head and threw me a condescending glance. I blushed, perhaps not beet red, and bowed my head, a habit I have acquired during many years of Japanese life.

Then the young woman shocked me.

"Eat it."

"Pardon me?"

"You can eat it here if you want to."

The two of them exchanged glances, smirking.

"No, that's fine. I'm sorry but I'd rather not."

I again bowed low, zipped up my bag and made my way, in a bit of a daze, between brightly lit duty-free displays to my gate.

The way I was treated in Sydney left a very bad taste in my mouth. Had I been a tourist, I might just have decided that it wasn't worth going back to that country. A similar thing happened to me in Tokyo, and I was actually grateful for the experience; and the loss in goods was much greater.

Good service is not only a matter of, to use the Japanese phrase,

"The customer is a god." It is the belief that if you are loyal to the customer in every way, the customer will be loyal to you. You are polite not because you are trying to get a customer to buy something, but because politeness is essential to the culture of service and you have taken on this culture as part of your duty of diligence.

I am constantly impressed when shopping in a Tokyo supermarket how a person working there will stop whatever they are doing to lead you to the place where the rice or the coffee or the soy sauce are. In every single country I have ever shopped in, what you usually get is a wave of the hand and an "over there," or, at best, "aisle five."

The last Kyoto house we lived in was built in the early Showa era. It had a beautiful courtyard garden adorned with a Japanese maple tree and an impressive old stone lantern. This house was located behind Vivre, the supermarket and department store, in a northern district of the city. In fact, it was directly opposite Vivre's parking lot.

There were cars going in and out of this parking lot throughout the day, and it wasn't always easy for us to back our car out of our driveway. But whenever we started to back out, the attendant at the parking lot, a middle-aged man in uniform and cap, would immediately stop all traffic going in and out of the lot, bow and wave us safely out of our driveway.

When we left this home to return to Sydney in 2001 we went to the attendant to say goodbye.

"It's going to be lonely without you here," he said.

We bowed to him and felt as if we were parting with a friend.

13

JAPANESE ORIGINALTIY

"The Japanese lack originality."

This is what a Japanese journalist said to me over dinner at a restaurant some years ago. It is a commonly held opinion among the Japanese people. (Or maybe he was fishing for a compliment to his culture from an "outsider.")

Hearing this I should have been polite and, as in a taidan, said, "I see. Of course I agree with you, but…." Actually I got all hot under the collar and said, perhaps thanks to having drunk some very delicious sake (Eisen, from Aizu Wakamatsu in Fukushima prefecture, and one of my favorite sakes), "What sort of a rubbish opinion is that!" Not in the least non-confrontational.

One thing can be said about the Japanese: They are, among nationalities, the people who may be the most blind to their own originality.

When did this myth of the absence of Japanese originality, of Japan being the copycat nation begin? Some Japanese faintly praise their fellow countrymen by saying they are skilled primarily at improving things. But the notion that the Japanese are only good at improving on the inventions of others is really just a glorified version of the "nation of copycats" myth.

This myth began in modern times, in the Meiji era, when all forms of Western culture were considered the obligatory accompaniment of development. Many aspects of Japanese culture were then seen as useless impediments to progress. If it hadn't been for the enthusiasm of Western artists and scholars, some of the most hallowed Japanese arts and crafts might not have survived. It is an ironical paradox that while Japanese artists of the Meiji era were obsessed with assimilating the practices of Western art, many Western artists—Van Gogh, Monet, Renoir and Whistler among them—were entranced by Japanese art.

A country's originality is based primarily on the rediscovery, reinvention and recreation of its own culture in each succeeding era. It goes without saying that countries open to the ideas and methods of foreign cultures will be stronger than those that continue to stubbornly inbreed. Japan's native culture has been enriched by assimilating influences from China, Korea, Russia, Western Europe and the United States. But the foundation of a country's civilization is built into the soil of its own native culture. The influences from the outside have only augmented the effectiveness of Japanese cultural forms.

Assimilation in Japan has not been just copycat imitation. It has involved the deep study of foreign cultures. The Japanese of the Heian period (794-1185) so immersed themselves in Tang Dynasty culture they became, for a time, more Chinese than the Chinese. Many artists and writers of the Meiji era were so Europeanized that they despised their fellow non-Westernized Japanese as hicks. And the Americanization of the postwar generation created a generation of people who love the trappings of American culture as much as or more than many Americans do. The Japanese are great assimilators, and this naturally leads people to assume they are copycats.

This assimilation in Japan has been but a transition to the recreation of something utterly Japanese. Eventually these foreign influences become so deeply entrenched in the Japanese psyche that they readily and often indistinguishably morph into something considered native.

There is another reason why many Japanese people seem to believe there is no originality here. True creativity in the arts is generally produced by rebels, iconoclasts, misfits, eccentrics and outsiders. People who defy orthodoxy are not readily accepted in any society, particularly a society like Japan's in which conformity to codes of behavior and decorum in public are vital aspects of social harmony. Japanese people do admire and even envy their rebels, iconoclasts, misfits, eccentrics and outsiders, but only, in many cases, after they become socially acceptable. The irony is that they end up creating a new orthodoxy to be challenged in subsequent generations.

The Japanese pantheon honors the names of scores of iconoclasts and eccentrics, from artists like Katsushika Hokusai to writers like Sakaguchi Ango and Miyazawa Kenji, from actors like Hayakawa Sesshu to scientists such as Minakata Kumagusu and Takamine Jokichi. These people were creative geniuses of phenomenal originality. And each in their own way was quintessentially Japanese in their relationship to art or science.

I have often wondered why the name Katsushika Hokusai is not known all over the world to the same extent as that of Rembrandt and Van Gogh. He is certainly as great an artist as any European old master. And yet European art still maintains the aura of universal value, while Japanese art is considered somehow special and exotic.

In the autumn of 2005 I walked in a trance through the massive Hokusai exhibition held at the Tokyo National Museum in Ueno, spending nearly three hours there. The works of this artist, who was known during his lifetime by some thirty different names, are brilliantly colored, masterfully drawn, witty, avant-garde even today and full of immense variety and outside influences (from China, from France, from Holland). The minute I left the exhibit I rushed to a public phone in Ueno Park, called Susan in Sydney and said breathlessly, "I'm so glad we came to Japan!"

There is everything in Hokusai, from the silly to the grotesque, from the mundane to the majestic, from the vulgar to the lyrical. European painters tended to concentrate on one or two types of subject, be it portraiture or landscapes, religious or mythical themes. Some, like Rembrandt and Breughel and Steen, painted ordinary people and scenes. But is there a master in Europe who so much as approaches the astounding variety of subject and method as Hokusai, influenced by East and West? This is what makes him supremely Japanese. This is a feature of the Japanese arts: Incongruous elements are tacked onto the whole until a new artistic medium of rich variety is created.

As a result, Japanese art is a jumble of styles and layers of themes. The openness of the Japanese to outside influences may, at times, make Japanese artists look like copiers or improvers. But this is only a part of a temporal process. Once these influences are absorbed, the result is something unique and striking. This is the form that Japanese originality takes.

Mid-twentieth-century author Sakaguchi Ango teaches us that the foundations of our culture are not material. They reside in the people at all times, ready to be produced with vigor and originality when the situation warrants. One of his famous dicta was, "I survive from here to there." He shunned possessions, spending most of his life living out of a suitcase that held his clothes and essential accessories. His passions and his implicit imagination were his true possessions. This he has in common with Hokusai, who didn't even own plates. Hokusai, like Ango, shunned fashion.

After the Great East Japan Earthquake in March 2011 I thought of Ango's words about us falling into the inferno of hell and then transforming the fire into blossoming flowers. Ango once wrote that it would do no damage whatsoever to Japanese culture if all of the temples and shrines of Kyoto and Nara were destroyed. If the people felt it necessary to rebuild them, either as they had been or in a new form, they would muster the creativity to do so.

Over the years I have written several books and many articles about Miyazawa Kenji, as well as translated his stories and poems. But one thing that constantly remains in my mind is a single image that speaks volumes about how he saw his place in the world. The image is that of a tree laden with drops of dew …

Whatever anyone says
I am the young wild olive tree
Dripping radiant dew
Cold droplets
Transparent rain
From my every branch

Kenji saw the human being as a single minute part of all creation. At a time in Japan's history when economic growth and the aggrandizement of national power were primary goals of his nation, Kenji was sending messages and signals to us in the twenty-first century, to harness the power of nature in ways that do not destroy it; to prosper and thrive economically, but to do it in a way that protects the integrity of our surroundings and the welfare of all people. In other words, development with compassion for all people and loving care to the natural environment. This was his loud and clear message to us a century ago.

The opening line of the above poem is telling. He knows that he is going against the grain of society, that people consider him an eccentric and a misfit. But he doesn't care. A person who does not fit into their society in one era may be the symbol of sanity and ingenuity in another. When Kenji tells us to be "strong in the rain," by rain he means all adversity, whether sent to us by nature or by our fellow human beings. He doesn't take it to heart when, as in the poem "Strong in the Rain," someone calls him "Blockhead."

I look to these Japanese people in the past to find out what they struggled against to create their genius and what elements of character they have in common. Certainly those elements consist in believing in oneself and one's gift, and not giving in to the trends of the time. The road to creating something truly original is never a smooth one.

Three people who in their own way displayed an amazing strength of will in the face of adversity were Hayakawa Sesshu, Minakata Kumagusu and Takamine Jokichi. All three fought their personal battles of achievement overseas as well as in Japan. It is much more meaningful for young Japanese to study the lives of these kinds of people in order to discover the keys to a successful and fulfilling life than for them to look to Thomas Edison, Madame Curie or Pablo Picasso.

What I want to stress is that these three Japanese forged their successes outside Japan, where the obstacles to a Japanese, or any non-white person for that matter, building a successful self-fulfilling career and making a contribution to humankind were much greater then than they are now.

Young Japanese people today have become, in a word, insular. This tendency has been highly criticized by the older generations. Yet it is those very older generations who created the inertia and stagnation that exists in Japanese society today. By trying to fault young people for a lack of ambition, they are only turning the gaze away from their own shoddy irresponsibility. Being insular may be a natural responsive behavior in today's Japanese society.

The origin of the word "insular" is the same as that of "island." When I first arrived in Japan in 1967 the term *shimaguni konjo* was very popular. It was used to explain and excuse a host of provincial behaviors. It literally means "the island mindset": We Japanese do not accept foreigners in our neighborhoods because of our island mindset; we do not speak foreign languages because we have an island mindset, and so on. To me it was nothing more than a lame excuse for prejudice. Instead of being tolerant toward outsiders, you blamed your intolerance on an abstract concept of national character and not on your own personal biases. Instead of making the effort to learn a foreign language, you blamed your intellectual laziness on some cliché about the insularity of your people.

The personal isolation and alienation of today's young people in Japan (described so clearly in the prose of Murakami Haruki) do not derive from insularity, nor are they masks for the ugly countenance of prejudice. Shimaguni konjo is today an obsolete phrase. The isolation and alienation derive rather from a sense of hopelessness: that no amount of personal effort will allow you to rise quickly in this society and make a mark on it. Why be ambitious when all you see before you is years of struggling conformity in a company? So you roll up in your little technological cocoon and seek personal fulfillment there. With contemporary technology you can explore the outside world and communicate with it without going anywhere. So, you *insulate* yourself and at least feel secure.

But remember that out of a cocoon, which is a case for a pupa, comes an adult who can naturally leave the insulation behind and fly away on its own. If young people today are in this cocoon stage, then let's consider them as being in pre-flight mode.

I first heard about Hayakawa Sesshu from my mother, who called him by his American name, Sessue Hayakawa. Sesshu had been the leading heartthrob in the silent movie era of Hollywood until Rudolph Valentino came along to rival him. Suave and handsome, he made a generation of young American women quiver and go all wobbly in the knees. The only trouble was that he was shorter than some of his American leading ladies. But Hollywood had a way of remedying this. They stood him on a wooden crate in scenes with the ladies. Eventually the term "to Sessue up" came into use for any movie hero who needed some physical "propping up."

Hayakawa Sesshu left Japan to study at the University of Chicago, but dropped out after taking only a course or two in his first year. He decided to try his luck in California, where he met the young actress Aoki Tsuru in Los Angeles and was himself discovered by film producer Thomas Ince. This began a meteoric career in film and on stage. At one point Sesshu had become a multi-millionaire in Hollywood, only to lose it all as a result of the jealousy of rivals, the perfidy of business partners and racial attacks on him. This was a time in the U.S. (the 1920s) of rampant anti-Japanese sentiment. Even in Japan he had many enemies who accused him in the early years of his career of bringing shame onto his nation in what were described as *kokujoku eiga*, or "films that insult the nation."

But Sesshu never gave up. He went to Europe and acted on the stages there. He returned temporarily to Japan in the 1930s, left once again for France, where he landed roles in film. He spent the war years in Paris, penniless and forgotten. It was only after the war, thanks to the intervention of Humphrey Bogart, who chose him to act with him in *Tokyo Joe*, that Sesshu made a comeback, subsequently appearing in David Lean's 1957 hit movie, *The Bridge on the River Kwai*.

By all rights Hayakawa Sesshu should be a household name in Japan, but I wonder how many Japanese people who can recognize

Marlon Brando and James Dean would see a photo of him and be able to recall his name. This is the point about originality in Japan. It isn't that there are no original creators in Japan. They are legion. It is only that the national character of the Japanese causes them to downplay the achievements of their own people. This is not a nation of hero worshippers like the United States. While such humility may be admirable, it should be recognized as humility and not truth.

Due to the many constraints on Japanese society, where people are expected to suppress the expression of their individual desires in the interests of social harmony, originality is not celebrated. This is not a society where people who call attention to themselves and their accomplishments are considered virtuous. But the Japanese virtue I am talking about in this chapter is originality itself, not the act of calling attention to it.

Hayakawa Sesshu's great gift as an actor and his inner strength as a human being facing prejudice and adversity combine to make him a remarkable Japanese creator of genius and an example to Japanese people of today of how to live out Kenji's advice of not giving in to the rain.

One of the most truly original thinkers of Japan—and one who speaks to us clearly—is Minakata Kumagusu. How did a person born in remote Wakayama in 1867 become a pioneer in his field of biology, recognized as such around the world? This is a time when Japan was still emerging from two hundred and fifty years of self-imposed national isolation, a policy that created a scientific and technological gap with the West of immense proportions.

And one more question: How could a man like Kumagusu, eccentric, feisty and volatile to the point of being wild, turn himself into one of the most respected, even worshipped, figures of the Meiji intellectual establishment? Here was a rare genius who *was* recognized in his time.

He represents the epitome of originality. He saw reality arising out of the co-mingling of *kokoro* (the spirit of things) and *koto* (the things themselves), and probed the realm where the two interlink.

He created an original view of reality by linking what he observed and studied with his personal thoughts and feelings. All great scientists do this. It was in this way that Albert Einstein created his theory of relativity, by *imagining* what reality was really like. Progress in science and invention in art both rely on the ability of the inventor to imagine a new reality from the given materials—facts in the case of science, ideas and images and sounds in the case of art—and formulate them in concrete terms.

Kumagusu was able to see all nature as interdependent elements, with the human being a single element in it. While he was very different in temperament from Miyazawa Kenji, these two thinkers share this wise view of reality. It is a view that we are just beginning to acknowledge and accept today. If you put humans above nature, as lord and manipulator, you will destroy nature to a certain extent and destroy human beings entirely. Nature will bounce back; we won't.

Kumagusu left Japan at the end of 1886 and didn't return until 1900, spending six years in the U.S. and nearby countries, and eight years in the U.K. Please look up the details of his amazing and colorful life, as scientist, as author of many articles written in English for prestigious scientific journals, and as an elephant driver's assistant in a traveling circus.

But the thing I admire most about Kumagusu was his fighting spirit. He was essentially as much a misfit in Meiji Japan as Miyazawa Kenji was in Taisho and early Showa Japan. Both Kumagusu and Kenji were activists. They did not sit in an armchair and preach. They took action according to their beliefs.

On August 11, 1910 Kumagusu barged into a meeting where officials were discussing the "development" of Wakayama timber, threw a portmanteau and a chair at some of them, and protested vehemently against the travesty of destruction they were wreaking on his beloved forests. Fanatic, yes; passionate and committed, absolutely. And where did this agitation opposing the greed and hypocrisy of much "development" get him? The police were called in and Kumagusu was arrested for breaking and entering. In court, however, he was handed a suspended sentence. After all, this celebrated native son of Wakayama had brought international renown to his prefecture. His pioneering work in slime molds, algae and fungi was recognized by the world academic establishment. He wrote as many as fifty articles for the British scientific publication, *Nature* (which was, in those days, a magazine of popular science).

His life, from 1867, the year before the Meiji Restoration, to 1941 (he died exactly three weeks after the attack on Pearl Harbor), spanned the greatest and most dramatic era of change in the last thousand years of Japanese history. His "three ecologies"—the ecologies of biology, society and the mind—teach us that the fundament of scientific research is a love and respect for nature. To Kumagusu, what the eye sees, what the mind reasons and what the heart feels are one. This total approach to reality symbolizes a very Japanese way of looking at the world.

When I was a little boy and I had a sore tummy, my mother would say, "Take a diastase." What I was swallowing for my tummy ache was a product known and widely used in the United States called "Taka-Diastase." My mother was saying "take a" instead of "taka," seeing as "taka" is not an English word. In fact, "taka" is a Japanese word, and it comes from the name of the scientist who invented the method of making this effective medicine still in use today in the United States.

Takadiastase is a kind of diastase made from the growth and development of *koji*. Koji is a fungus used in the manufacture of soy sauce and miso. Its Latin name is Aspergillus oryzae, and it has been designated as a "national fungus" in Japan. Countries have national flowers, but I have never heard of any other country having a national fungus.

The man who, in 1894, invented the method to extract the digestive enzyme takadiastase is Takamine Jokichi. Little did I, or my mother, know that I was swallowing a product invented by a Japanese scientist. Takamine Jokichi is one Japanese who should have, by all rights, received a Nobel Prize in Chemistry. He was the first person to isolate adrenalin.

Born in Takaoka, Toyama prefecture, in November 1854, Jokichi spent his childhood in Kanazawa. The story of how he studied in Glasgow; went as co-commissioner of the Cotton Exposition to New Orleans in 1884, where he met his future wife, Caroline Hitch; and spent his life making such important discoveries that by all rights he could be called the father of biotechnology, or at least one of the fathers, forms one of the most fascinating biographies of a Japanese in the modern era. And yet, how many young Japanese know his name or know of his world-class achievements?

Jokichi's mother was violently opposed to the marriage. The young couple went to live in the United States, but Jokichi was barred from taking U.S. citizenship, even though his wife was American. The racist laws of the time prohibited it. In addition he often encountered virulent racism, the kind of racism that turns particularly vicious when white people see themselves challenged by successes on the part of non-whites. Envy and racism are a deadly combination. Racists don't so much mind when they see people they hate who are destitute or failing. It reinforces their prejudices and helps them feel superior. But they loathe members of "inferior" races who succeed, because that success disproves their perverted theories.

When Jokichi was working in Peoria, Illinois, trying to convince people there that koji could be useful in the beer industry, the labor unions were not well disposed to this "Oriental." The distillery was burnt down in what was probably an arson attack, though this was never proven. Jokichi lost a great deal of money from the fire. He was facing the same obstacles in Illinois that Hayakawa Sesshu would in California.

Despite these hardships he persevered with his discoveries and patents, eventually succeeding once again. He and Caroline built a Japanese mansion in Sullivan County, New York. In 1912 he put up the money to have some two thousand cherry blossom trees sent to Washington, D.C., where they are now a famous symbol of beauty and friendship between Japan and the U.S.

Jokichi died in July 1922 and is buried in a mausoleum at

Woodlawn Cemetery in New York. There is a stained glass window in the mausoleum picturing Mt. Fuji.

Of all of the photos of Jokichi I have seen, my favorite is one taken in the sumptuous garden at Shofuden, his and Caroline's mansion. Jokichi looks dignified and imposing in traditional Japanese dress, which he often wore even in the United States; and Caroline, wearing a kimono, is standing on a raised area beside a large stone lantern. Life must not have been easy for these two people, who were, it is said, madly in love with each other. Despite the era and the trials of invention and investment, Takamine Jokichi stands as a monument of perseverance and originality in a very Japanese manner.

We can read the biographies of a hundred famous people and still not know what makes them representatives of a particular nationality or era. We must look for the traits that allowed them to succeed. I have chosen only a few of the many original Japanese I admire in order to discover what it is in them that makes them Japanese and what we can learn from them to help us create a Japan where originality and creativity are stimulated and encouraged in the future. This is the key to the rebranding of Japan as a force in the world.

It is clear that Japanese people have the right spirit to create and invent, and when the times are a catalyst for that spirit, there is nothing to stop this country from becoming a beacon of creativity to the world.

So, how do we create such times?

The answer is to encourage young people to challenge us, even to defy us. As strict and constraining as society was in the Meiji era, people did recognize that society had to create the breathing space for its original minds, so that they could stray from the mainstream and create new tributaries and channels.

The freedom to be different, to *not* fit in, is vital for all creativity. It is the kind of freedom that the older generations of Japan today are reluctant to sanction. They are the ones stifling initiative in commerce and education, and the politicians who are subsidized by them are reluctant to create regulations that would free innovators, particularly in the energy industries, to change the face of Japan.

Kenji wrote that everyone had to imagine the universe in their own way and then follow the consciousness created by that imagination. Young Japanese should be telling themselves this: "My view of the world is unique, and it is my own. I have been given a life in order to act in compliance with this unique view."

This initiative is the source of genuine originality, that what you produce and create in your life—or the very way you live your life—comes out of you, from the kind of person you are, from your thoughts, your feelings, your desires, your aspirations and your character.

We may not all be able to be like Hokusai, whose originality was manifest and richly variegated into his late eighties, or like Meiji author Higuchi Ichiyo (1872-1896), who managed to write the most extraordinary short stories despite the incredible handicap of being a poor woman in a society totally dominated by men. We may not possess the iron will of a Sesshu, a Kumagusu or a Jokichi. But we can express our originality in our jobs and in our relationships with people. You don't need to have a test tube or a pen or a brush or a violin in your hand.

You just need to believe that the world needs what you wish to give.

14

"THIS STRANGE LAND"

Stand up, young man.... Stop fighting little battles....
Learn to keep this strange land properly in your mind.

These words were written in 1935 by the woodblock artist Fujimaki Yoshio and published in issue 16 of the magazine *Shin-Hanga* (The New Print) under the provocative title "Live your era ... Surmount your era." What a stunning title! We should both live in our era and transcend it at the same time.

Born in 1911 and, sadly, not at all well known today, Fujimaki produced writings on art and life as profound as his art is beautiful. I like the phrase above, very wise for a man of only twenty-four. Alas, five months after this was published, on September 2, 1935 to be exact, Fujimaki disappeared from the face of the Earth. No one, to this day, knows what happened to him. He simply vanished into thin air.

How can a single individual, of whatever age, sex or status in life follow their conscience and still be a respected member of society? How can a person live "properly" in "this strange land"?

A country changes continually. What is correct and acceptable today may be frowned upon and shunned tomorrow. People who are outside the mainstream of "proper" behavior or ahead of their time may suffer greatly, despite the fact that what they do will be judged both proper and correct in the future.

This is a dilemma that faces people in all countries, not only Japan. When you see an injustice being done and have the chance to bring it to the attention of others, do you act on it? Do you get involved personally and expose this injustice, even though you personally may have nothing to gain from it? You may even be denounced and denigrated for doing it. Your actions may harm your position or the status of your job, as, say, when you blow the whistle on someone who is acting in an underhanded or illegal manner. If you are the partner of just such a whistleblower, do you support your partner, even though their actions may endanger the status of your household? If you live in a country or city with a corrupt leader, do you protest, and if so, what means of protest do you adopt?

Each of us is presented with difficult personal decisions, and it is not always easy to do "the right thing." You may be praised in the future for your ethical stance, but we all live first and foremost in the present. How can we bring together our present interests with those of ourselves and others in the future? How can we be decent good people who help others, even when we ourselves "get nothing out of it"?

A man who faced just such a dilemma, at a time when his decisions affected the lives of thousands of people as well as those of his family, was Sugihara Chiune. Chiune is a person who kept his country properly in his mind ... and heart.

I was fortunate to have known his eldest son, Hiroki.

"My father chose my name," he told me, "in honor of Hirota Koki." (Hirota Koki was prime minister in 1936, the year that Hiroki was born.) Sugihara Hiroki was a kindly and soft-spoken man, dedicated to perpetuating the memory of his father as a righteous Japanese.

The image that the world has of Japanese men at the time of the war is one of unrelenting cruelty and a total lack of compassion for anyone seen as an enemy. It goes without saying that one cannot blame nonJapanese people for thinking this of a particular generation of Japanese, given the record of brutality left by the Japanese military from that time.

Sugihara Chiune—often called "Sempo," an alternate reading of his given name that he made a point of using because it was easier for foreigners to pronounce—stands as a virtuous model for us all, especially because he lived in an era when the Japanese model was perverted and degraded.

What is the meaning of the word "conscience"? The answer is that its definition depends on the cultural context of the country.

To religious people in the West the very word "conscience" suggests a Judeo-Christian ideal. The conscience is a primarily religious entity to people of faith in the West. To some Christians there is no such thing as conscience outside of the framework of Christianity. Those who adhere to no faith at all cannot, by definition, have a religious conscience and therefore cannot truly tell right from wrong. Yes, they may do good things in their life, but that is because all of God's children are capable of good. Even believers in other religions and atheists are, whether they know it or not, "God's children."

Now, it is true that Sugihara Chiune had become a Christian. He converted to the Orthodox Christian faith, feeling strong affinities with the culture of this faith. He cherished those affinities for his entire life. His first wife, Klavdiya, was Russian. In fact I believe that he felt closer in some ways to Russians than he did to his own Japanese people. After all, he chose to live the last decade and a half of his life primarily in the Soviet Union. (Sempo was said to be the best speaker of Russian in the Ministry of Foreign Affairs. It was this linguistic skill, too, that probably saved his life.)

But it was not as a Christian that he acted, nor, I dare say, as a Japanese, but simply as a human being who made a personal choice on what he considered the right and moral thing to do.

Before I go into the powerful act of individual conscience demonstrated by this man, let me fill you in on its background.

The end of the Second World War found Sugihara Chiune, his wife, Yukiko, and their little children in Romania, interned there by the Red Army. It was unclear what their fate would be. Japan had been officially at war with the Soviet Union for only a matter of days before the war ended on August 15, 1945, and this made the Sugiharas enemy aliens.

Sugihara was a diplomat who had been posted to the Japanese consulate in Kaunas, Lithuania, in November 1939. He was soon to be presented there with a striking dilemma.

"My father woke up one morning in late July 1940 to see a great crowd of people milling outside the gate of the consulate," Hiroki told me in July 2000 in Tokyo. "I remember staring down at them from the second-story window. They were Jews, and they had come to get exit visas from my father."

Sugihara was under strict instructions from his superiors at the Ministry of Foreign Affairs in Tokyo not to issue any Japanese visa other than a transit visa, and this only when the applicant had a valid visa to a subsequent destination.

Sugihara deliberately disobeyed those instructions, issuing more than two thousand visas, some of them covering more than one member of a family, to Jews who were desperate to escape the Nazi terror that had overtaken Poland and was gradually moving eastward. (Some of the people he saved came from east of Kaunas, sensing that they were unsafe in any region vulnerable to Nazi occupation.)

"The consulate was shut down," said Hiroki, "but my father continued to pen visas at the railway station, throwing the last stamped passports out of the window of our train to Jews whose lives would, thanks to him, be spared."

The refugees saved by Sempo traveled by train across Siberia and on to Japan, from where they eventually made it to Shanghai, Australia, the United States or other destinations. Incidentally, those Jewish refugees were treated humanely while in Japan, despite general Japanese sympathies for the Axis cause. The Japanese authorities and people were not anti-Semitic; and despite the hardships that they themselves were living under, they dealt with these Jewish refugees fairly and compassionately. Owners of some bathhouses opened their doors to Jewish refugees free of charge.

Meanwhile, Sugihara, with his family, made his way from Kaunas to posts in Prague, Konigsberg and, eventually, in 1942, Bucharest, where he remained until 1945.

Why did Sugihara go out on a limb to save those Jews? It wasn't an obligation of his job. If anything it was an obligation not to assist them. Sugihara's son, Hiroki, saw his father's actions as a matter of personal conscience.

"My father made a decision based on pure human conscience. If you had the power to save people and didn't, what kind of a man were you?"

Sugihara Chiune himself spoke years later of how moved he was by the plight of these desperate people, pleading with him, weeping before him with their wives and children. How could he do otherwise?

That is the question you must ask yourself: How can I do otherwise? At such times, there is only one answer, though it requires immense courage, often at your own possible peril, to make: I could not do otherwise.

Sugihara, his wife and their children, were freed by the Red Army and found themselves on the same trans-Siberian train line ridden by the Jewish refugees he had saved. They were finally repatriated in April 1947. Two months later Sugihara was relieved of his duties at the Ministry of Foreign Affairs in what some have interpreted as a rebuke for his disobedience. This explanation fits into the stereotypical view of the conformist Japanese and of a bureaucracy that allows no flexibility for the individual or freedom of choice. But I believe this was not the case here. Instead, Sugihara was simply let go in the postwar changing of the guard that saw a third of the Ministry's staff receive their marching orders in those chaotic years. It is the case, too, that the Ministry of Foreign Affairs itself, its reputation badly damaged, wished to take collective credit for his good deeds as a matter of postwar damage control. Perhaps, too, Sugihara was seen as being too old fashioned in his viewpoints, too much like a prewar Japanese strategic diplomat. This was certainly true of many diplomats who were made redundant. In any case, I doubt that Sugihara himself desired to stay in the foreign service.

After leaving the Ministry he found various jobs, one of them at a PX on an American base. Eventually he took up a position with a trading company and moved, alone, to Moscow, where he lived in all for some sixteen years. Born on January 1, 1900, Sugihara Chiune passed away in Japan on July 31, 1986.

"I think that my father may have felt more comfortable with Russians than he did with Japanese," Hiroki told me. "I guess he wasn't very much at home in postwar Japan."

There are tens of thousands of people around the world today who would not have been born had it not been for the compassion of Sempo Sugihara. Not all of the Japanese people who were active during wartime were devils (though there certainly were a host of them). There were angels in their midst. In 2000 a monument was erected in his honor at his hometown, Yaotsu in Gifu prefecture, on the centenary of his birth.

Sugihara Chiune's eldest son, Hiroki, died of stomach cancer, age sixty-four, in June 2001. He had spent some years at a college in Sacramento, California and chose to settle, in 1996, in nearby San Francisco. I had met him on his trips back to Japan.

Back in the early 1980s I had an encounter with a man who became innocently involved in an international incident. This incident has been all but forgotten. But there is a reason for bringing it up again, because it highlights the struggle of a man of conscience in his attempt to have the truth revealed.

In 1981 the Japanese sociologist and progressive thinker Hidaka Rokuro was invited to two universities in Melbourne Australia, La Trobe and Monash, to conduct research and teach. But unexpectedly the Australian government refused to grant Professor Hidaka an entry visa.

I heard about this visa refusal and, incensed, immediately contacted the editor-in-chief of Melbourne's influential daily newspaper, *The Age*, informing him. A few days later we broke the story on the front page, causing this to turn into an international incident.

Despite letters of support from, among others, Governor of Kanagawa prefecture Nagasu Kazuji and famous political scientist Maruyama Masao, and despite the fact that it was the Japan Foundation sponsoring the visit by Professor Hidaka and his wife, Nobuko, Australia's Department of Immigration and Ethnic Affairs not only withheld a visa but refused to explain why. I set out to expose this visa refusal for what it was: an unjust decision by a kangaroo court of ill-informed bureaucrats.

I discovered that the visa refusal stemmed from an incident in France in 1974, when the Hidakas were living there. In September of that year Nobuko was taken in for questioning by the French police. (Professor Hidaka had gone back to Japan in May 1974.) She was not charged with any crime and released by the police, after which she returned to Japan to join her husband.

It appears that some months previous to that she had rented one of the rooms in their Paris home to a Japanese scholar of French, and this scholar had, from time to time, received visitors. Nobuko never met any of these visitors. But a newspaper reported that one visitor was a member of the Japanese Red Army, the militant group that had perpetrated violent acts in the Middle East and elsewhere.

The Australian government was claiming that Professor Hidaka and his wife were active supporters of the Red Army, even though there was no evidence to back this up and the French police had concluded that the Hidakas were not involved in any way with this radical organization. The absurdity of the government's decision was blatant. Anyone in Japan or elsewhere who knew the Hidakas considered it preposterous that they could possibly be accused of such activity.

The Australian government dug in their heels, accusing Professor Hidaka's former students of association with the Red Army and refusing to reconsider the denial of a visa to Australia. A small group of supporters, including well-known scholars Sugimoto Yoshio and Gavan McCormack, kept up pressure in the media. And, when the Labor Party came to power in 1983, the new minister reconsidered the application and granted him a visa.

"The Japanese side wasn't as persistent in support of my case as the Australians were," Professor Hidaka told me after the visa was granted in 1983. "The Japanese don't have much of a consciousness of human rights or the rights of the individual. Even the word *kenri* is not really the equivalent of 'rights.' The Japanese think that insisting on your kenri is an activity associated with egoism."

The "Hidaka Affair," as it was known, ended well, and Professor Hidaka visited Melbourne in 1983. But involvement in it backfired on me in Japan when Professor Hidaka and I published a taidan in the *Asahi Journal*. Another Japanese magazine that had previously commissioned an article contacted me to say that they weren't going to run it, though it had already been written and submitted by me.

"Why not?" I asked. "Wasn't it good enough?"

The editor remained silent, and that was the last I ever heard from him. Subsequently I was told by a friend in the know that they axed the commissioned article because "we don't want to run a piece written by someone who supports a terrorist."

In other words the Japanese editor had acted exactly like the minister in Australia, judging me guilty of something on the basis of hearsay and fabricated rumor. And this was already some time after the entire affair had blown over and Professor Hidaka was vindicated.

As I look back at this incident I have tremendous admiration for Professor Hidaka. Why did I get involved myself in this? I had never met him before this incident occurred. It was out of personal anger at this injustice. I am not a particularly brave person, and generally do not get involved in other people's problems. Maybe that is one reason why I fit in so well in Japanese society. But I had no choice in this case. My personal sense of what I knew to be right was violated.

Hidaka Rokuro, scholar and author of major postwar books on Japan's role in war and peace, passed away at a nursing home in Kyoto on June 7, 2018, age one hundred and one.

Earlier I wrote about my dear old friend Wakaizumi Kei. He took a stance on the basis of conscience, not out of anger but out of a sense of remorse and guilt of what he had done in betraying the people of Okinawa. Like Sugihara Chiune, his conscience told him that this was the only course of action open to him.

Well, it's fine for famous people like Sugihara Chiune, Hidaka Rokuro and Wakaizumi Kei to act in a righteous manner, but what about the ordinary citizen? Ordinary people are not faced with such challenges of conscience in their lifetime ... or are they? I believe, actually, that we are faced with many such choices in our daily life. How we react to them goes to define our character.

There is a particular practice in Japan inimical to the fostering of individual conscience. If this practice can be eliminated, then I think Japanese people will have a much clearer sense of what the Japanese word for "rights" means. Let me explain by starting with a question.

What do these Japanese people have in common: A neighbor of people whose house has burned down; a relative, friend or colleague of someone who has been in a car accident; a person who has been the victim of some injustice?

The answer is that they are all likely to appear headless on Japanese television, perhaps with their voices altered to such a high pitch that they sound as if coming from the squeeze box inside a stuffed koala. Even victims in Japan are sometimes considered in some way at fault for what happened to them.

All Japanese channels, government-run and commercial, claim to have stringent rules about the protection of people's privacy. But these rules are abused through excessively zealous application. I know of no other developed country where witnesses to events appear so often in such a state of decapitated incognito. It used to be that their faces were blurred out. Then, during the 1980s, the people interviewed on television whose identity was deemed "compromised" bore a countenance made up of little mosaic squares, somewhat in the style of the cubist paintings of the early twentieth century.

In July 1996 what became a very severe and widespread case of E. coli O157 food poisoning broke out in Sakai City, Osaka prefecture. More than 6,500 people (some have put the figure at nearly double that), primarily elementary school pupils, were affected due to their consumption of tainted pre-cooked lunches.

Television stations naturally inundated the airwaves with news of this public health disaster, and many people directly and indirectly affected by it were interviewed. Food poisoning is a common occurrence in Japan, where much food is prepared in advance and is sometimes left to sit unrefrigerated for hours. Yet although there was no criminal intent on the part of those who prepared the lunches, the children who fell ill, their parents and even unaffected people who lived near them appeared on TV from the neck down or in an altered depersonalized mosaic-like state.

The assumption was that they did not wish their identity to be known for fear of being associated in some way with misfortune, and that anonymity was the best protection against calumny in a country where guilt by association reigns throughout the society.

I recall a TV report of a waiting-room scene in one of the hospitals that was treating the patients. While the reporter spoke of the suffering that the children were going through, the entire scene behind her was distorted into a milky blur. Ironically, however, a scene of the very same waiting room appeared clear as crystal in a CNN report carried on the NHK satellite news channel. There was no effective way, I suppose, to impose Japanese "standards" on a foreign broadcaster.

What is at work here? Is it really that Japanese people regard it as an invasion of an individual's privacy to show them in a news broadcast, even when they are in no way compromised by the appearance? Do people who consent to interviews about some accident, for instance, truly object to being visually identified? Or does the media actually encourage this form of censorship in order to lend an aura of titillating conspiracy to a news item?

It goes without saying there are many cases where a person's identity should be legitimately protected. Victims of crime or whistleblowers are often interviewed on the BBC, for instance, sitting with their backs to the camera or in dark shadow. But in Japan the TV blurs the face or cuts off the head, thus hiding the identity, of people who are not in any danger.

This blatant policy of non-identification goes well beyond

the demands of either privacy or propriety. In addition, what is essentially a coverup of reality turns the news into a conspiracy of whispers. News reports come to resemble the pseudo hush-hush entertainment of variety shows, where reporters sneak around famous people's homes whispering into microphones and making provocative accusations into the intercoms at their front gates.

Unless there are real issues of privacy or potential harm to people, all interviews should be conducted openly and in full view of the public, with any person not wishing to appear on TV obviously retaining the right not to be seen. If that person accedes to an interview, however, then let them appear with their head on their shoulders and speaking in their normal voice.

Your opinion or your comment on an issue comes from your thoughts and your personal experience. It must not be presented anonymously. If you say your opinion about something without giving your name or showing your face, then that opinion carries no responsibility in a democracy. It is worthless.

If there is a lesson to learn from the past of Japan or any country, it is that each citizen must speak and act according to their own conscience, standing by the decisions they make. Of course, these decisions may turn out to be wrong. At such a time you must take responsibility for your decisions by apologizing or making amends. If you deny your responsibility or try to blur out your role or do what is called in Japanese *nasuri-tsukeru*, or shifting the blame onto someone else, then you are not acting according to your conscience.

This is an ideal for Japanese young people to strive for. They can look to the past of their country for many examples of people who stood up for what they believed in and took responsibility for their actions. Doing this is a sign of strength, not weakness.

If Japan is to succeed in reshaping its mores to fit the needs of this century, then the Japanese people must opt for openness. This entails freeing up the flow of information between people, knowledge-sharing across disciplines and institutions, and social dialogue that crosses the lines of gender, class and ethnic origin.

The old model of the smoothly operated well-oiled machine of Japan, where the manual is kept secret and everyone remains silent in the face of injustice, has run out of steam. Knowledge and information are not a gift. They are the individual's right to have and share.

I do feel that the younger generation of Japanese is not as fearful of letting out secrets or airing their views publicly as their elders are. Once you open up to others, you gain their trust, and they, in turn, open up to you. The winner is the entire society. News is truth; truth, news.

Having a conscience is not the monopoly of one religion or culture. All people in the world are the same in this. We all have the ability, if not always the clear choice, to do what we deem right.

I say to young Japanese: Don't be afraid to show your face, as the true face of a new Japan, to the world.

15

A NEW CONSENSUS

The 1990s delivered the Japanese people a triple punch. The first was the punch to the belly in the form of the puncturing and shriveling of the economic bubble. Then a body blow came on January 17, 1995 when the Great Hanshin Earthquake struck Kobe and nearby districts, killing nearly 6,500 people. Finally the uppercut: the sarin gas attack of March 20, 1995 on the Tokyo subways, perpetrated by an occult radical religious sect, Aum Shinrikyo.

Susan, our four children and I had returned to Japan in December 1994 to live in Tokyo. We told our friends and relatives that we wanted to go back to Japan because it was a safe country to bring up children. Within three months the safety myth of the country was shattered, first by a natural disaster and then by a manmade one.

Could the new generation just continue to enjoy their indulgent MASK culture and take refuge in their latest toy, the Tamagotchi, the digital pet that seemed perfectly suited to a generation of self-contained little pleasure seekers, people who seemed more comfortable spending time with electronic goods than with their peers? Could the old generation solve the unprecedented problems facing Japan with the "proven" Japanese tools of nose-to-the-grindstone, single-minded stick-to-it-iveness, when few could express clearly anymore what was worth sticking to?

The entire value system of this country was shaken to its foundations by the events of the 1990s, and, in a sense, Japan has not recovered. A further devastating blow was dealt Japan's confidence by the unprecedented Great East Japan Earthquake, tsunami and the subsequent catastrophic failure of the Fukushima Daiichi nuclear facility.

Well might we ask: How can Japan recover and reinvent its

values for the future? The answer is that this process of reinvention began more than two decades ago and has been proceeding ever since.

Things began to change in the mid-1990s, although the changes, as is often the case in Japan, began in the subculture, below the surfaces that are generally recognized and described by the mainstream media, Japanese or foreign.

First, the subculture of the young who had immersed themselves in the appurtenances of personal satisfaction altered its direction to take in the needs of others. Thousands of young volunteers flocked to Kobe and its environs to help the victims of the earthquake. They were not asked. They needed no incentive imposed on them from above. They just felt the personal need to go and they went. They brought great comfort to the survivors of the earthquake.

Second, many practitioners of social sciences turned their attention away from mainstream society—the salaryman being its anointed chief representative—to those who had long been discriminated against: women, children, the elderly, the disabled and ethnic minorities such as the Koreans living in Japan since before the war.

Third, the media itself began to wise up. When I was on TV talk shows in the 1980s the pervasive message of discussion was that Japan was problem free. "We are a society," said one famous commentator, who will remain anonymous, "with no child abuse, no sexual harassment and none of the big social problems faced by people in the West." It sounds like an arrogant boast today, but at the time most Japanese people believed it because the media and the people's own dread of calumny kept them in the dark.

From around the mid-1990s, however, serious roundtable TV talk shows began exposing the troubling extent of domestic violence against women and children, bullying in schools, sexual harassment in the workplace, and institutionalized discrimination against the disabled. Japan was not spiritually immune from social evil. Japan was a "normal" country with grave and rampant problems.

Finally, artists were highlighting social problems in their work.

The first production of Inoue Hisashi's play about Hiroshima and its aftermath, *Chichi to Kuraseba* (*The Face of Jizo*) was staged in Tokyo in September 1994. This is a play that treats the nuclear holocaust of August 6, 1945 as a personal problem for all Japanese citizens. Playwrights like Sakate Yoji and Nagai Ai were staging popular plays covering a gamut of issues, from whaling to the suppression of dissent in schools. In 2007 Suo Masayuki exposed the major problem of being falsely charged for a crime in his film *I Just Didn't Do It*. The Japanese police are so concerned with pinning a crime on someone and so proud of their nearly 100-percent conviction rate that they frequently and deliberately frame the wrong people and go to great pains to stick to their guns, even years and decades after the people are languishing in prison for crimes they didn't commit.

What began as cultural degeneration in the late 1940s and early '50s, and morphed into regeneration in the '60s, '70s and '80s, has turned into a reorientation on the basis of a set of values that had not existed in Japan before. This set of values says that individuals can seek a high degree of personal satisfaction while still showing concern for the needs and problems of people outside their family or ethnic circle.

For the first time Japanese people were not only sympathizing with strangers but seeing their own interests to be in concert with those of strangers, be they people of a different age group, gender, physical ability or ethnicity. What is still beyond the horizon is the new national goal itself, one to replace economic growth for its own sake, one that will provide a paradigm to aim for, namely, the creation of a society inclusive of all people living in Japan and a dedication to their welfare and their quality of life.

My feeling is that the Japanese people are on their way to crossing the horizon and finding that paradigm. The new goals will necessitate the reorientation of business in harmony with ecological preservation and resource conservation, and the creation of ethical entrepreneurship; the pluralization of values and the expanded tolerance for alternative Japanese lifestyles that comes with it; and the establishment of enforceable rights of minorities.

If there is to emerge a new consensus among Japanese people on both domestic and international matters it will be based on this model of enlightened self-interest, mutual respect, compassionate cooperation and tolerance.

What needs to be done now to achieve this?

Consider, if you will, four words. The nation's take on these may decide the future of Japan. They are: race, nationality, ethnicity, and citizenship.

Actually these words do not lend themselves to clear-cut definitions or translations. They overlap. But they all add up to what we call our identity. Identity may seem to be one consistent thing, but it is really a vessel containing a multitude of identities that come from the above four concepts, as well as from religion, gender, sexual preference, age, etc.

Race is a meaningless word in the twenty-first century. What race are the Japanese? Oriental? If they and other Asians are Oriental, then why do we call Japanese prejudice against Koreans or Vietnamese prejudice against Cambodians *jinshu-sabetsu* (racial discrimination)? What am I? The term that describes my race is "Caucasian" or "white." But this only describes the purported color of my skin; and I do not come from the Caucasus. Does skin color define race? Of course it doesn't. It just indicates the pigments your skin has. This notion of race was devised by people with white skins who wanted to use it to claim superiority for themselves over people with darker skins.

Nationality refers to one's nation, and the word nation is related linguistically to the verb "to be born." Your nationality is generally identified by the place or ethnic group you are born into. After the creation of the modern nation-state in the nineteenth century, people began associating nationality with their country. But in reality nationality is a narrower concept. We speak of the Navaho nation. The Navaho, native Americans, do not have their own country. But Navaho people claim Navaho nationality. Certainly being a Kurd means having a Kurdish nationality.

Ethnicity is a newer term denoting the cultural or religious group you belong to. The dictionary that defines this as a factor of "race" is out of date.

Citizenship is entirely a legal term. It describes the country or countries whose passport you hold. Many countries allow multiple citizenships. Japan as yet doesn't, but in the future this is bound to change, considering the large number of people today who have parents of differing nationalities or who divide their time between countries, and in fact do hold more than one passport.

Now, to the vast majority of Japanese people nationality, ethnicity and citizenship are the same: Japanese. They have never felt the need to distinguish among these. But take my case, for instance. I was born and raised in the United States and I consider my nationality to be American. I am Jewish by ethnicity, even though I do not believe in God. Ethnicity in my case is a cultural identification. My only citizenship is Australian. I gave up my American citizenship in 1976. In my case the three things are different. If you wanted to describe my identity, it would have to include all three: Jewish, American and Australian, not to mention the one I personally identify with most, Japanese.

Is that confusing? It might be confusing to most Japanese, but it certainly isn't to me. I feel no inner conflicts over this whatsoever.

How does this apply to Japanese people in the twenty-first century? I wrote earlier about the five Japans. Does this have any effect on the question of nationality, ethnicity and citizenship? It absolutely does. Japanese people are bound to redefine their identity in terms of the way they come to view themselves. By doing so the Japanese will not only enrich the possibilities for development in the country but will also enhance their understanding of issues and conflicts around the world. Japan has begun—thanks to the changes set in motion in the 1990s and an increased public awareness of problems around the world and how they relate to Japan—to become a genuinely pluralistic and multi-ethnic society.

There has been, since the 1990s, a subconscious widening of the notion of what it means to be Japanese. Gradually, I believe, people's notion of national identity is changing, and the old single criterion of blood has less significance than it did before. For instance, foreign athletes, or those of mixed Japanese and nonJapanese identities, have come to represent Japan; and Japanese people are taking pride in their achievements.

Many children are being born to one Japanese parent and one nonJapanese parent. Are these children Japanese? Of course they are, if they identify themselves as such, even if it is only one of their nationalities. If they don't identify as Japanese, they are not. And what of an ethnically Korean person whose ancestors have lived in Japan for three or four generations? Are they Japanese? Yes, if they call themselves Japanese. They are Korean Japanese; but they may choose not to identify themselves as such if they feel no tie either linguistically or culturally with Korea.

In other words, your identity in Japan is gradually developing into something that depends on how you view yourself, not on how others in society view and judge you. This is a major reorientation transpiring in Japanese society today. The self-awareness of the Japanese as a pluralistic and multi-ethnic nation has actually been developing for two decades now.

There is a phenomenon in Japan today that can be called "domestic cross-culturalism." It highlights the recognition that people from Okinawa and Tohoku, for instance, while being Japanese in nationality and citizenship, may be ethnically different from Japanese born, say, in Tokyo or Kyoto. The culture and history of these regions of Japan have shaped the ethnicity of the people there so that they think, act and talk differently from people in other regions. It does not make them any less Japanese. It simply provides another element that adds to that Japaneseness and by doing so enriches the definition. The era of Japan as "the homogeneous nation" is over.

These shifts have definitely been occurring since the 1990s and will form, I believe, a new cultural paradigm for the future of Japan.

I have written in this book that a strong vibrant and spirited Japan is a necessity to the world. Japan is the world's foremost secular democracy. Matters of faith and concepts of otherworldly spirits play virtually no part in the political decision-making process in Japan, as they do in the U.S., some European countries, Australia and even, if ideology is seen as a kind of faith, in China.

This has not always been the case in the past 150 years. Japan, too, once chose the course of establishing a national religion, State Shinto, based on ancient rituals and nationalistic rhetoric. It then used this to fuel the engine of imperialism roughly from 1895, when the Sino-Japanese War ended in victory for Japan, through to 1945, when the Second World War ended in capitulation.

In that period an entire spiritual tradition was created, rationalized and codified by Japan's ruling elite in order to mobilize the nation in the cause of empire building. That "tradition" of Bushido, often termed "the samurai spirit," was not a philosophy, let alone a practical code of ethics. Shinto was never a religion in the sense of providing a moral guide to behavior. The emperor had not been, until Emperor Meiji was restored to the throne in 1868, a hands-on unifier of the nation-state.

And yet, all of this was promulgated and imposed on the nation as if it had existed since time immemorial in those very forms. In other words, the Japanese people were hoodwinked into believing that there had always been some spiritual force pushing them toward supremacy in Asia and the Pacific. After several decades—certainly by the mid-1930s—the once-formidable opposition to this historical mythmaking was crushed. The result: Millions of people were killed and maimed in the name of what was no more than a trumped-up nationalism. State Shinto, Bushido, emperor-worship: These had nothing whatsoever to do with morality or ethics, Japanese or otherwise. They were a cloak to hide the greed of the Japanese elite who manipulated the nation and held a dagger to the people's throats for the aggrandizement of its status and empowering of its class.

After the war State Shinto was defrocked; Bushido was emasculated; and the emperor went back to being a peaceful and un-divine symbol. Japan was once again a secular state. It was in this context that the Japanese people diligently and civic-mindedly rebuilt their nation.

Japanese culture is a medium that makes the country perfectly poised to play an intermediary negotiating role in a world where Christian and Muslim values are clashing. Japanese people, by keeping faith out of their everyday lives, respect all religions and have no religious axe to grind themselves. The Japanese can stand in the middle and provide a safe place for negotiation between the Christian and Muslim worlds.

Japan has also merged Chinese Confucian culture with libertarian Western culture, producing a workable balance of the two. The logical role for the Japanese in this century is to be a sagacious medium between the United States and China, defusing cultural and ethical problems that exacerbate geopolitical ones. Japan may be the only country that can stand between the two superpowers of the twenty-first century and mediate conflict between them. In order to do this, however, the Japanese must establish the kind of trust that the Chinese people will accept. This requires a full and honest assessment of Japan's role in Asia in the first half of the twentieth century. Without that candid public assessment, Japan will be stuck forever between two giant stools, rushing from the feet of one to the feet of the other, ultimately viewed with suspicion by the occupants of both.

Clashes of faith and ideology are bound to continue to plague the world. The Japanese, with neither religious nor ideological agendas, have a crucial role to play in ameliorating the distrust on both sides that fuels those clashes.

The 1990s in Japan, with their physical and ethical crises, were not the lost decade. They will one day be seen as the first decade of substantial change in the values and the very identity of the Japanese people. This can form the basis of a new paradigm for Japan, one that encompasses compassion, understanding and the willingness to get along with its neighbors.

Once again, I feel we can look to Kenji's thoughts on what each individual can do to revitalize a society. Kenji's deep understanding of the human's place in society and the world provides us with a secure guarantee for sustainable social design.

The most telling example in recent years of how Japan failed to secure that guarantee is seen in the nuclear disaster triggered by the Great East Japan Earthquake and tsunami of March 11, 2011. Viewing the catastrophe through the eyes of Miyazawa Kenji puts it in perspective.

Kenji was born in 1896, the year of the Meiji Sanriku Earthquake. He died in 1933, the year of the Showa Sanriku Earthquake. Both of those natural calamities gave rise to gigantic tsunami in the very coastal regions of Tohoku devastated once again in March 2011. In fact the 1896 tsunami produced more deaths, some 22,000, than the one in 2011. Had we been aware of this and turned this awareness into rejection of nuclear power generation on that very coastline, we would have avoided the catastrophe of radioactive substances being spread throughout the land and into the water, ruining the livelihood of hundreds of thousands of people.

A few lines from the poem "Scenery and the Music Box" give us a lyrical and profound description of the human place in nature. If we view our place in nature in this way, then we may think twice before acting to degrade it ...

A farmer rides his horse
Finding half his body fusing
With a clump of trees and its silver-atom surroundings
He is quite amenable himself to this fusing

The farmer on his horse is blending into the dramatic landscape of Iwate. More than blending, he is half melting into it. The poem allows us to see the farmer as a physical element that is an essential part of the natural landscape. After all, we now know that the same particles coming from distant stars formed both us and the landscape.

In this poem Kenji is cutting trees from the mountain, but he knows that the mountain may take revenge on him for this. He is obliged to replant trees to replenish the land for what he has taken and implores the hill not to be angry ...

Be still, be still, Goken Hill
Be still though your trees have been cut out of you

Kenji was also a world pioneer in the field of animal welfare. He was obsessed with the well-being of animals long before this theme was taken up by other authors in the world. Nearly a century ago he wrote a story titled "The Frandon Agricultural School Pig," the hero of which is a Yorkshire pig who refuses to be slaughtered. Kenji became a vegetarian at age twenty-one and considered animals as the equals to humans in their ability to feel and suffer.

As we look over his entire body of work, we find a writer with a keen sense of the fragility of nature's balance and one who sees the human being not as the lord of creation but rather as a single element whose existence depends upon that of all phenomena. We discover the issue of animal welfare, as well as other issues at the forefront of social responsibility in our century, such as the climate crisis and renewable energy. Kenji addresses the need to replenish nature that we have exploited. He was passionate about economic development, but only if it caused no permanent damage to nature.

Kenji tells us that the cosmos is both very far away and, at the same time, right by our feet. Here is a passage from his poem "Koiwai Farm" that merges distance and time in our everyday reality ...

What's wrong with my being
A carefree forester
A white duffel bag hanging loosely off my shoulder
Striding along, whistling a tune
Through the radiant golden light of May?
Oh this joyous solar system spring!

Spring in the solar system, discovered on a walk through a

modern farm close to home. What could be more symbolic of our place in the universe?

The decisions that Japanese people take on development and the generation of energy today will affect everyone in the world. Miyazawa Kenji was that rare Japanese who pointed it out to us, a twenty-first-century visionary born in the nineteenth century, a supernova that exploded in September 1933.

The light is just beginning to reach us now. Let us hope that some of this light shines over the road that Japan will take.

I am full of hope for the future, so long as Japanese people recognize the time when the growth occurring now in the subsoil flowers for all to see.

It is at that time that they will rethink their ideals and create lifestyles and humanistic ethics relevant to the twenty-first century.

16

THE GIFT OF JAPANESE DESIGN

A stopped watch has no more value than the price of its metal.
—Kitaoji Rosanjin

The great gift that Japan has given the world is the gift of design.

I am talking here about the verb "to design," which means to fashion in the mind and invent; to formulate or devise a plan for something; to plan out systematically in graphic form; to create for a particular effect or in an artistic manner. Japanese design carries all of these meanings and nuances.

When Japan opened its doors to the outside world at the end of the Edo period, people overseas, particularly in Europe and America, but also in China, immediately became bewitched by the culture of Japan. This is because Japanese culture not only masterfully fuses the abstract design of objects with their construction but also encompasses space and time in it.

A Japanese meal is not just a blending of flavors. Its very presentation is a theatrical design of the passage of time, from one dish to another, a combination of colors and textures that take you through the meal as if you were on a journey. The presentation of the meal regulates the way you eat it.

The fascinating thing about the plates of Onta and Koishiwara in Oita prefecture is that the brush is brought down many times onto the plate as it spins on the wheel. This produces dynamic lines that show movement, just as in cursive Japanese calligraphy you can see the movements of the brush in the India ink. The passage of time is captured and expressed on surfaces.

One feature of Japanese aesthetics that redesigns time is *totsuzensa*, or suddenness. Japanese culture is full of the unexpected and the unpredictable, what Kanze Hisao called "revelations." This links up with the theatricality of gesture that I discussed earlier. In kabuki or bunraku it can take the form of an instant transformation from one state to another. In Edo-period woodblock prints that depict kabuki actors it is evident in the poses and grimaces, capturing a startling instant of drama.

Kobayashi Issa's haiku illustrates how incongruity and suddenness create drama ...

A swallow shoots
Out the nose
Of the Great Buddha

No one designs time like Miyazawa Kenji, who set the stage for his poetry in his "Preface to Spring and Ashura" by writing ...

The propositions that you have before you are without exception
Asserted within the confines of a four-dimensional continuum

Kenji sensed that you cannot properly describe the present without incorporating what transpired in the past and what is likely to occur in the future. One of his key metaphors is that of Buddhism's Indra's net. We are connected to each other and to all natural phenomena by the threads of this colossal net. Droplets of dew rest on each thread; and in these mirror-like droplets we see not only ourselves but beyond ourselves. We observe the reflections within droplets of dew behind, in front of, to the left of, to the right of, above and below us. In other words in a single vision we see all creation, and not only as its exists in space but as it is stretched out in the long mirror of time. In Kenji's world, the past, present and future of here and everywhere exist simultaneously.

The importance of this for Kenji is that it speaks of our interconnection and interdependence with all things at all times. It is the consciousness of this vital link that informs us of the need to live within, not outside, nature and to consider the welfare of the whole as a prerequisite for our survival. Our fate hangs on each thread, no matter how far away it is from us.

It is not a long leap from this viewpoint of humanity and its surroundings to the precepts of Japanese architecture. Japanese architecture has designed space ingeniously, merging the outside with the inside. Contemporary architect Kuma Kengo inspires us with his assimilation of the natural environment into space and onto surfaces. The way Kuma designs and redesigns water in his guesthouse in Shizuoka prefecture is stunning. It is not by accident that this house is located next to one designed by German architect Bruno Taut. An atmosphere of peacefulness—of time caught in and stilled by space—that is present in Kyoto's Katsura Detached Palace, whose aesthetic beauty and simple elegance Taut praised, is present in Kuma's guesthouse too. Kuma's books, *Nature's Architecture* and *Anti-Object*, are among the best treatises of Japanese aesthetics for our day that I know.

The Japanese garden is essentially a redesign of landscape in a confined space. The absence of the nonessential is the key to the simplicity of the design. Japanese opulence is shibui, or understated. It is this seeming contradiction, of understated opulence, that has both puzzled and overwhelmed artists, designers and architects in the West for the past century and a half.

Japanese aesthetics redesign the scale of space as well. Again, it is incongruity and the innate asymmetry of Japanese beauty that come into play in two of Issa's haiku ...

How beautiful!
The Milky Way from a hole
In my sliding rice-paper window

A frog in the evening croaks
Lining up its bottom
With the top of Mt. Fuji

Both of these haiku offer images that redesign the spatial relationship between things. What is big? What is small? It all depends on your perspective and your personal viewpoint. The logic of perspective is absent. In fact sometimes absence itself defines a space. There is a genre of traditional Japanese painting called *rusu-e*, or "absent pictures." These are paintings in which no humans appear. The title of the genre throws the attention onto the viewer, who becomes the introduced observer in the frame.

It is by no means only Issa who deals in such incongruity. The spatial stretch of the imagination is present in many poets' poems. Two of Masaoka Shiki's haiku portray small animals in a big picture ...

The snail is enticing
Rain clouds
With its antennae

The red dragonflies are swarming
Over Tsukuba
With not a cloud in the sky

I would define haiku as "the redesign of space and time in seventeen syllables." By redesigning space in this way, Japanese culture places humans properly in nature, as only one small element among a multitude.

The design of time and space in Japanese culture in this way has given Japanese people the breathing space to slow down and wait patiently for things to transpire. It even affects the way people speak, in using pauses and moments of silence in expressing themselves.

Needless to say, much of this slow pace of life and the pattern of observance of things has been lost in Japan. But it still exists in the culture of the country and can be retrieved and recreated for people's lifestyles once again.

The design of the erotic is another element in Japanese aesthetics. Even though this is a society where decorum, propriety and prudence play a very big part, there is not a religious sense of shame connected with the body as there is in the Christian West. It may be shameful to show the body but it is not a sin. It may seem a paradox, for instance, that there are no public nude beaches in Japan as there are in most countries of the West, and yet the culture is dripping with erotic imagery. It was the Meiji sense of morality, borrowed in large part from Victorian England, that changed a very bawdy Edo culture into a publicly prudish modern Japanese one. The old ribald culture, however, is still alive and kicking under the skin.

This paradox struck me when I visited the Hokusai exhibit in Ueno. The museum shop sold two versions of the catalogue, one in Japanese and the other in English. They were alike in all ways except one. The English version contained Hokusai's shunga (erotic pictures) and the Japanese version didn't.

The poetry of Yosano Akiko is unique in the world for its time and its openness toward the body. The kind of frankness and honesty expressed by Akiko in some of the poems in her most famous collection of tanka poems, *Midaregami* (*Disheveled Hair*), symbolizes a Japanese design of the erotic. Could any female poet in any country have written a poem like this more than a century ago?

I press against my breasts
Gently parting
The shroud of mystery
Revealing the flower
Redder than red

Or this …

"Spring doesn't last," I said to him …
"You don't believe in permanence, do you?"
And I took his hands in mine
Leading them
To my young full breasts

Or this!

> *My blood burns*
> *To give you one night*
> *In the shelter of heightened dreams*
> *God, do not look down on one*
> *Who passes through spring*

What more lovely metaphor for the ecstasy felt by one "passing through spring" could there be than the shelter of heightened dreams?

The design of the erotic, the grotesque and the theatrical was taken to an extreme in the work of an artist whose work I deeply love, the man named Hirose Kinzo but known as Ekin.

After being implicated in an artwork forgery scandal in 1844, perhaps innocently, perhaps not, Ekin wandered the Shikoku countryside painting for dyers, kite makers and other such artisans. It was when he turned his hand to painting screens that his genius emerged. His enormous screens depict scenes of high drama, catching people at an emotional, and sometimes orgasmic, peak. Grotesque, yes. Full of gore, even more so. His screens scream out theatricality in raucous colors. This is Breughel and Dali rolled into one, but even more provacative. Anyone who might believe that Japanese aesthetics are all understatement and minimalism should have a look at the works of Ekin. This is the epitome of lavish Japanese theatricality—the overstatement of emotion.

Perhaps all of this adds up to what might be called "The Design of the Unknown." Surely the elements of suddenness and incongruous spatial relationships, the grand flights of time, the potent mixture of the erotic and the grotesque, the instant switch from the understated to the overstated, are very evident in Japanese manga and anime, which have had and are continuing to have such an influence on world culture. What is the world of animator Miyazaki Hayao if not the design of the unknown,

THE GIFT OF JAPANESE DESIGN

that Kenjiesque jumbling together of the past, present and future? (Kenji's influence on Miyazaki is evident in many of the animator's work, particularly in his masterpiece, *Spirited Away*.)

The influence of the Japanese design aesthetic, beginning with the opening of Japan to the outside world around the middle of the nineteenth century, has been incalculable.

Shirasu Masako is a person who spent the latter half of her life devoted to examining and propagating that aesthetic. How she came to be a proponent of Japanese culture is an amazing story in itself.

"If you use beautiful things every day," she wrote, "you will naturally cultivate an eye for beautiful things without giving it a second thought. In the end, you will be repelled when you encounter the ugly and the fake. If only all Japan would come to see this, how much more joyous our lives would be and how genial and gentle people would be!"

Few Japanese live a life in closer contact with everyday beauty than the woman who penned these words. I suspect that no Japanese author has as much to tell us today about how to revitalize a culture trapped in the cul-de-sac of value stagnation.

Shirasu Masako published more than fifty books during her lifetime, though she did not start writing in earnest until she was in her early thirties. Her complete collected works, published by Shinchosha in 2001-02, now include more than sixty books, not counting those co-authored. She defined the tastes of postwar Japan in almost every aspect of Japanese aesthetics and design. Yet despite the immense erudition underpinning her principles and the uncommon elegance of her style, she was totally lacking in pretense and affectation.

Writing in a notebook in 1947 she remarked, "I believe, without a doubt, culture to be something that exists in the life of every single person as a part of their life from one day to another. Being faithful to yourself and becoming engrossed in your work, *that's* culture."

Her evolution from pampered little princess to Japan's premier advocate of the simple, the austere and the unadorned in Japanese art brings to light a remarkable story.

Shirasu Masako was born on January 7, 1910 in a mansion at Nagatacho, Tokyo. Both of her grandfathers were admirals in the Japanese navy. It was just two and a half years before the death of Emperor Meiji, and Japan was on the cusp of monumental change both domestically and internationally. Cultural and political democratization were to be the hallmarks of the Taisho era that followed, and the Japanese people aspired to be the equals on the world stage of the dominant European powers. And yet the society itself had only half-emerged out of the hard shell of the feudalism that had restricted its progress for centuries.

Masako had a foot in both camps from a very early age. At four she began taking lessons in the noh theater, a ritualistic performance art that had come to be the symbol of staid refinement during the Edo period. When she was fourteen, she became the first female to perform on a noh stage. At the same age, she left Japan to enter school in the United States.

She studied at the Hartridge School (now the Wardlaw-Hartridge School) in New Jersey. Hartridge was known as a girls' prep school for Vassar College. Her experiences there and at summer camp in Massachusetts among the privileged classes of the United States turned her into a cultivated and fluent speaker of English. But this life wasn't to last long.

Her father, a man of stalwart morality and, apparently, unending generosity, lost his money in business, and Masako was forced to sail back to Japan in 1928. Curiously, another bankruptcy, that of the father of Shirasu Jiro, also saw the young son returning to Japan from Cambridge University in the U.K. that year. Masako and Jiro met and were married the next year. She was nineteen.

Jiro, born on February 17, 1902, was over six feet tall, devastatingly handsome and a man of highly sophisticated Westernized tastes. He had been sent to the U.K. after graduating middle school and had immediately taken to the lifestyle of the country gentleman (this is how Masako later described him), driving a Bentley around town and racing a Bugatti on weekends. (Virtually up to the end of his life in 1985 he drove his Porsche about the Japanese countryside.)

When, shortly after the war Jiro was appointed by Prime Minister Yoshida Shigeru as Councillor of the Central Liaison Office and given the task of being go-between for Yoshida with Gen. Douglas MacArthur, Supreme Commander of the Allied Powers, Masako called him "a straightforward obstinate samurai," a fitting adversary to the pontifical general. As deputy head of the Economic Stabilization Agency Shirasu Jiro played an instrumental role in laying the groundwork for Japanese postwar economic recovery. He worked, for a time, for the *Japan Advertiser*, an English-language newspaper absorbed by the *Japan Times* in 1940.

But Masako and her obstinate samurai both realized as early as 1940 that Japan was destined to lose the war in Asia and the Pacific. Concluding in 1942 that Tokyo was bound to suffer mass destruction, they purchased a dilapidated thatched-roof farmhouse near Machida, then a village located away from potential targets in Tokyo. There, at least, they could grow their own food while they waited for the war to end. They collected butterbur sprouts, Japanese ginger and Japanese parsley from nearby fields, ate the bamboo shoots from their backyard garden and baked bread from homemade flour.

"When we left the city the word *sokai* (evacuation) was not yet in use," she wrote in *Shirasu Masako Jiden* (*The Autobiography of Shirasu Masako*), "and anyone who escaped from Tokyo was labeled a traitor."

It was the experience of living in the farmhouse, I believe, that transformed Masako, instilling in her the sense of what is absolutely necessary to survive in body and spirit. After all, the Japanese aesthetic is founded on the bare essence of all things.

Not long after the war she met brilliant men such as Kobayashi Hideo, Japan's foremost literary critic; antiques guru Aoyama Jiro, about whom she subsequently wrote a book; and Kon Hidemi, author and, from 1968, the first director of the newly-created

Bunkacho, or Agency for Cultural Affairs.

Masako blossomed as a fiercely original essayist on all subjects relating to culture. Late in life Jiro wrote of her, "My old lady is amazing. Everyone else just reads about a place without going there, but she always sets out to wherever it is even just to write a few pages about the place. No one does that anymore."

When Tokyo was hosting the Olympic Games in 1964, she left the capital for Shikoku, to walk the island on a pilgrimage to its many temples. She visited scores of out-of-the-way places in Japan to view old noh masks. These masks are primarily held in private collections, and owners are reluctant to send them away for display. In preparation for her ground-breaking study of the old temples and stone art in rural Nara, *Kakurezato (Hidden Village)*, she made monthly trips to the area over a period of years and trod every path there.

The key to understanding her passion for Japanese art is precisely here, in the rough beaten paths leading to it ...

"As the noh theater has its *hashigakari* (bridge to the stage) and the kabuki its *hanamichi* (runway from the stage through the auditorium)," she wrote, "life's charm is not a result but rather the journey toward a result."

She saw Japanese art, in all its spare simplicity, as an unending process toward natural imperfection. In her book *Nihon no Takumi (The Ingeniousness of Japan)* she wrote of the renowned Iga-ware potter Fukumori Masatake: "He hates being called an *auteur* or a ceramic artist, and never uses the term 'work of art' when talking about his pots. The reason why he became so interested in food is because he wanted to create the plates to put it on."

In other words she was attracted her entire life to the very act of creativity, focusing on the creators and their pure relationship to their materials. Speaking of the craft of dyeing, but applicable to all the arts, she wrote, in 1947, "What we need is not artists but artisans. People attempt to create art and fail. If you create something with great skill, it may very well result in art."

She went so far as to view nature through the lens of its having been fashioned by those artisans. She professed a passion for things that displayed an artless (*ubuna*) art. She loved the phrase *hana o ikeru* (arrange flowers) because of its connotation of bringing flowers to life (ikeru can also mean "living, being alive").

"The fleeting nature of the flower," she wrote, "is brought to life for the first time as the perfect harmony of stillness and movement, immutability and fluidity, because of the vase it's in."

There you have it: It is the artificial container that gives life to nature as a medium to experience something spiritual and profound. The message is contained in the art of the vessel. Nature gives rise to art, and art illuminates it in return.

She spent more than half a century after the war probing the relationship between nature and art, concluding that "There is nothing in the world as all-encompassing as Japanese nature. Religion, art, history and literature are latent within it."

She was a superb dresser drawn to the craft of fabric making, in her later years favoring clothes designed by Missoni. She travelled extensively around Iran, France, Spain and Hungary. She was a lover of Japanese cuisine who said, "Eat what you feel like eating all the time. Those food connoisseurs and gourmets who glow with self-satisfaction give me the creeps." At Katsuragi, in Nara prefecture, she went straight back to the very roots of Japan's culture, from the time before influences from China and Korea swayed it. "Nothing stirs the human imagination as the primeval natural landscape and faith as found in Katsuragi," she wrote in *Kakurezato*. And yet her library of some ten thousand items, preserved at Buaiso, her farmhouse home near Machida, has a great many books relating to world culture, from texts in Latin to Proust and Gide, from Dostoevsky to *Elle*.

Shirasu Masako died on December 26, 1998, and is buried at Shingetsuin temple in the city of Mita, Hyogo prefecture, beside her husband, Jiro, who predeceased her by thirteen years.

She stands as a prime and perfect symbol—I will go as far as to say, a beacon of light—for the coming decades in Japan, where a renewal of the spirit is the sine qua non of social and economic regeneration. I think she should appeal to young Japanese people, this fascinating and free-spirited woman who wrote, "Looking back, it seems that I've spent my whole life dawdling by the wayside, from one road to another. ... I may have lost something on the way, but I think I have gained more. ... The appreciation of art is not a process of folding one's arms, viewing and listening to the explanations of others, but rather of participating in the acts of the people who create it."

Finally, there is the Japanese language itself to consider as an element of design.

The Japanese language was, for a long time, considered by the Japanese as a tool of communication that could truly be used only among Japanese people, a kind of code language that could really be understood solely by the Japanese people. In recent decades, however, hundreds of thousands of nonJapanese have studied and come to understand and speak Japanese. I published a book in 2014 in Japanese, *The Wonder That Is Japanese*, dispelling the myth that the Japanese language is difficult to learn to speak. If the Japanese continue to believe that their language is somehow uniquely hard to learn and understand, reinforcing some racial stereotype of separateness that they harbor about themselves, they erect a barrier not only to non-native speakers of Japanese keen to assimilate but also to their own abilities to understand the outside world.

The internationalization of the Japanese language is one of the best things that has happened to Japan in the past four decades. Let me tell you of a personal incident that may bring this to light.

Back in the 1980s I used to meet from time to time for lunch with a French sociologist friend. My French is poor, and his command of English is not very good, so naturally we spoke in the only language we shared, Japanese. Like me, he had been living in Japan for many years.

We agreed to meet at a French restaurant near Tokyo's Nogizaka Station, not far from fashionable Roppongi. I arrived first. The restaurant was packed with people, all Japanese. Luckily I had booked a table for two. I sat down at the table, which was located

THE GIFT OF JAPANESE DESIGN

right in the middle of the restaurant.

After a short while, my friend appeared, rushing to the table and excusing himself in Japanese. We exchanged pleasantries and sat down, continuing our discussion, first about our wives and children, then about various other topics that I have now forgotten. But it didn't take long for us to notice that a hush had fallen over the restaurant in which about thirty other people had been noisily chatting away only moments before. Not only that, most of the people were staring directly at us. How is it, they must have been wondering, that two foreigners are talking to each other in Japanese? I tell you, we had no privacy at all during that lunch and had to speak to each other in whispers.

Now, I realize that such a scene was rather exotic for the Japanese in that restaurant. But why should it have been? When I travel around the world I often see and hear non-native speakers of English from many countries in Asia, Europe, Latin America and Africa speaking English with each other. I do not find this exotic, and I certainly am not going to sidle up them and listen in on their conversation.

To add insult to injury, when my French friend and I finished the meal, we fought over who was going to pay the bill at the cash register. Now not only the guests at the restaurant but all the waiters were staring at us in amazement, no doubt thinking, "Why are those two *gaijin* (nonJapanese) acting in that way, as if they were Japanese?"

The fact is that we in the West, and I suspect people all over the world, also consider it polite to be generous and pay for a meal for our friends. We were not being Japanese. We were being human.

That is why the internationalization of the Japanese language is a good thing for Japan. It shows the Japanese people that much of the kind of behavior they think particular to themselves is actually universal; and that the Japanese language, as a tool of communication, can be used by all people in the world to speak with each other. It's just another one of the world's approximately 6,500 languages, and it can be mastered by non-native-speakers who have the curiosity and will to do it.

But there is another element to the Japanese language that I would like to bring up in this chapter on culture as design. I see the Japanese language as a design medium for Japanese thought and emotion. It is this element of the language that cannot be understood by nonJapanese people unless they have a thorough knowledge and appreciation of Japanese culture and society.

Over the years I have been told countless times by Japanese people that Japanese is an ambiguous language. This misconception by the Japanese reinforces the notion that they are somehow uniquely mysterious in this world. But, no language is inherently ambiguous or vague. It is possible, of course, that a certain nationality will couch some of its expression in a purposely vague manner, giving the impression of ambiguity. This does not make the language itself ambiguous. All languages are neutral territory. If a Japanese person uses a phrase that appears vague to someone from the outside, that does not automatically make it vague. The criterion of the presence or absence of vagueness or ambiguity is this: Does the person being spoken to clearly understand the meaning or intent of the speaker? If there is understanding on both sides, then the phrase used is not vague or ambiguous. If you understand the cultural and ethnic background of a language, the alleged ambiguity disappears.

The words of Fujimaki Yoshio come back to me, that it is important for Japanese people to imagine and re-imagine this "strange land" in their own way, for them to appreciate the universality of their culture and to keenly desire people around the world to become familiar with it. That is the only way Japan will surmount this era of lethargy and inaction.

I quoted master potter, master chef and superlative designer Kitaoji Rosanjin at the top of this chapter. A timepiece, like a culture, is not an object created to be kept in a drawer and cherished. It has got to move ahead to have value.

Young Japanese people in the twenty-first century are perfectly capable of getting that timepiece going again by redesigning Japan first and, by doing so, contributing to a redesigned world.

But first they must take to heart those words of Akashi Kaijin: "If you yourself do not burn like the fish who live in the depths of the sea, there will be no light anywhere."

AFTERWORD

I began this book on the banks of the Kitakami River in September 2008. A wind passed through me as I stood there. That wind carried a message. It was a message that I didn't really understand myself until the events that began on March 11, 2011 struck Tohoku and reverberated around Japan and the world. Those awful and horrendous events of destruction signaled a change in the mindset of the Japanese people. Those events must be the catalyst that eventually urges the Japanese to change direction and establish a model of growth based on the respect for nature.

Only a lifetime's instant before September 2008 I had been riding in a taxi from the airport into Tokyo. That was September 1967. It wasn't the wind then, it was a plate of glass—the taxi window—through which I observed the lights of the city. Those lights carried a message too. It was a message that said to me, "You are starting on an adventure. May your adventure be exciting and fulfilling. May your journey be long and full of fascination. The goal is the journey itself."

I had no idea what kind of a person I was going to be in the ensuing years, who I would marry, whether I would have children or not, or even what my life's work would be.

Young people today are being forced too early into making decisions. There is no need to decide on the direction of your life at an early age, though if you do happen to do this, that's fine too. But do not just drift like a piece of driftwood on the surface of the sea. Sink down into that sea and observe everything in it. Turn yourself into a sponge at the bottom of the sea and absorb whatever comes your way. Then recall Akashi Kaijin's advice and burn with a bright light.

The moment I looked out that taxi window into a kaleidoscope of light, I chose to stay and live in Japan, and that changed my life. It did more than change my life. Japan made me the person I am today.

It eventually led me to the best advice for the twenty-first century, though it came from a person who was born at the end of the nineteenth century. It is Miyazawa Kenji's "Strong in the Rain." I began this book with Kenji, and so it is perhaps fitting to end with words that he left us.

Strong in the rain
Strong in the wind
Strong against the summer heat and snow
He is healthy and robust
Free from desire
He never loses his temper
Nor the quiet smile on his lips
He eats four go of unpolished rice
Miso and a few vegetables a day
He does not consider himself
In whatever occurs ... his understanding
Comes from observation and experience
And he never loses sight of things
He lives in a little thatched-roof hut
In a field in the shadows of a pine tree grove
If there is a sick child in the east
He goes there to nurse the child
If there's a tired mother in the west
He goes to her and carries her sheaves
If someone is near death in the south
He goes and says, "Don't be afraid"
If there are strife and lawsuits in the north
He demands that the people put an end to their pettiness
He weeps at the time of drought
He plods about at a loss during the cold summer
Everybody calls him "Blockhead"

AFTERWORD

No one sings his praises
Or takes him to heart ...

That is the kind of person
I want to be

About the Author

Author, playwright, theater/film director and translator, Roger Pulvers's novels include *The Death of Urashima Taro, General Yamashita's Treasure, Star Sand, Liv, The Dream of Lafcadio Hearn, Half of Each Other,* and *Peaceful Circumstances*. He has also published numerous works of nonfiction, collected essays and translations from Japanese, Russian and Polish. Roger's plays have been performed extensively in Australia, Japan and the U.S. He has twice directed at the Adelaide Festival of Arts in Australia and at major theaters in Japan. He was assistant to director Oshima Nagisa on *Merry Christmas, Mr. Lawrence*. In 2016 he wrote the screenplay for and directed the film of *Star Sand*, which was released throughout Japan in 2017. Prizes and honors include the Crystal Simorgh Prize for Best Script at the 27th Fajr International Film Festival in Tehran, the Miyazawa Kenji Prize and the Noma Award for the Translation of Japanese Literature. In 2018 he was awarded the Order of the Rising Sun, and in 2019 the Order of Australia.

About the Cover

Alice Pulvers was born in Tokyo, Japan in 1984 and has lived in both Tokyo and Kyoto. She is bilingual in Japanese and English. Alice's work is deeply influenced in its composition, perspective and color by her absorption of Japanese culture during her early life and subsequently on visits back to Japan. Alice has created covers and illustrations for several books and has been a finalist in numerous art prizes. Her work can be seen at www.pulvers.co

www.ingramcontent.com/pod-product-compliance
Lightning Source LLC
Chambersburg PA
CBHW031105080526
44587CB00011B/838